Everyman's Poetry

Everyman, I will go with thee,
and be thy guide

William Cowper

Selected and edited by MICHAEL BRUCE

Goldsmiths College, University of London

EVERYMAN
J. M. Dent · London

This edition first published by Everyman Paperbacks in 1999
Selection, introduction and other critical apparatus
© J. M. Dent 1999

J. M. Dent
Orion Publishing Group
Orion House
5 Upper St Martin's Lane
London WC2H 9EA

Typeset by Deltatype Ltd, Birkenhead, Merseyside
Printed in Great Britain by
The Guernsey Press Co. Ltd, Guernsey, C. I.

British Library Cataloguing-in-Publication
Data is available on request

ISBN 0 460 87991 X

Contents

for Peter Dixon

Note on the Author

WILLIAM COWPER was born on 15 November 1731 at his father's rectory in Great Berkhamsted, Hertfordshire. After a conventional education at Westminster School, there was a desultory flirtation with the law. Yet Cowper was ill-fitted for the cut and thrust of the legal profession. Instead, he read poetry, wrote light verse, and fell in love with his cousin Theodora: a relationship terminated by parental veto. In 1763, faced with public examination at the House of Lords, Cowper collapsed in nervous panic, attempted suicide, and was taken to an asylum at St Albans. For Cowper, this was the end of any engagement in public life. During his rehabilitation there was some form of evangelical 'conversion', and, on leaving St Albans, he took lodgings in Huntingdon with the Revd Morely Unwin. When the minister died, Cowper and the widowed Mary Unwin removed to Olney, Buckinghamshire, the parish of the Revd John Newton, with whom Cowper would later write the Olney Hymns (1779). For the next three decades, he adopted the role of retired country gentleman. Ostensibly, the years passed in passive quietude, yet it was an equilibrium easily upset by debilitating bouts of depression. Mundane tasks provided therapy, but most effective was his return to poetry in the early 1780s. The first collection, *Poems by William Cowper of the Inner Temple, Esq.* (1782), was dominated by the so-called 'moral satires', and met with a muted critical response. Much more successful was the publication, in 1785, of *The Task*. There was recognition by reviewers that Cowper had achieved something original, both in writing about the domestic, daily round of rural living, and in the unforced 'naturalness' of his language. He seemed to catch, if not predict, the spirit of the times, and to find among his admirers Wordsworth, Coleridge and Austen comes as no surprise. His last major enterprise was the translation of Homer (1791), but unhappily, by now, Cowper's mental health was rapidly deteriorating. While attempting to recuperate in Norfolk, he died on 25 April 1800.

Note on the Editor

MICHAEL BRUCE was born in Surrey and educated at King's College School, Wimbledon, Fitzwilliam College, Cambridge and Westfield College, London. He is now Lecturer in English Literature at Goldsmiths College, University of London. He has published on the pastoral tradition, and on neo-classical literary theory, and has a particular interest in representations of the English countryside in eighteenth- and nineteenth-century poetry. In the Everyman Poetry series, he has also edited the poems of Jonathan Swift.

Chronology of Cowper's Life

Year	Age	Life
1728		John Cowper, DD., Rector of Great Berkhamstead, chaplain to George II, marries Ann Donne
1731		15 November, Cowper born
1737	6	12 November, mother dies. At Revd William Pittman's school in Markyate Street, Bedfordshire
1739–40	8–9	Living with Mrs Disney, an eminent oculist, having developed an eye complaint

Chronology of his Times

Year	Literary Context	Historical Events
1727	Dyer, *Grongar Hill* Gay, *Fables* Pope and Swift, *Miscellanies*	George I dies. George II succeeds to the throne. Newton dies
1728	Gay, *Beggar's Opera* Pope, *Dunciad* (i–iii) Swift, *A Modest Proposal*	
1730	Fielding, *Tom Thumb* Thomson, *Seasons* Goldsmith born	
1731	Defoe dies Pope, *Epistle to Burlington*	
1733	Pope, *Essay on Man* (i–iii), *Epistle to Bathurst*	Walpole's Excise Scheme
1734	Pope, *Epistle to Cobham*	
1735	Pope, *Epistle to a Lady, Epistle to Arbuthnot*	Copyright Act
1737	Green, *The Spleen* Shenstone, *Poems on Various Occasions*	Licensing Act subjects plays to censorship by Lord Chamberlain. Queen Caroline dies. Prince of Wales heads opposition
1739	Hume, *Treatise of Human Nature*	War with Spain
1740	Richardson, *Pamela*	War of Austrian Succession
1741	Arbuthnot *et al.*, *Memoirs of Scriblerus* Fielding, *Shamela*	

Year	Age	Life
1742	11	Enters Westminster School, 10 April
1745	14	Translates an elegy (now lost) by Tibullus, poet of the Italian countryside
1747	16	Last year at Westminster. Friends include Vincent Bourne, a fifth-form master whose Latin poems Cowper will translate; also Charles Churchill, the satirist; Robert Lloyd, the poet; George Colman the Elder, the dramatist; Walter Bagot and Sir William Russell
1748	17	Leaves Westminster. After several months at Berkhamstead Cowper is admitted to the Middle Temple. First extant poem written: 'On the Heel of a Shoe', modelled on Philips's *Splendid Shilling*
1750	19	Articled with Mr Chapman of Holborn. Spends time with his cousins at the house of his uncle, Ashley Cowper, in Southampton Row

Year	Literary Context	Historical Events
1742	Collins, *Persian Eclogues* Pope, *The New Dunciad* (Book IV of revised work) Young, *The Complaint, or Night Thoughts* Fielding, *Joseph Andrews*	Walpole resigns: Carteret in ministry
1743	Blair, *The Grave* Pope, *The Dunciad* (final version)	George II present at England's victory at Dettingen
1744	Pope dies Akenside, *The Pleasures of Imagination*	Carteret falls: Pelham ministry. France declares war on England
1745	Swift dies Akenside, *Odes on Several Subjects* Thomson, *Tancred and Sigismunda*	Charles Edward Stuart (the Young Pretender) wins Battle of Prestonpans
1746	Blair dies Collins, *Odes*	Charles Edward defeated at Culloden
1747	Gray, *Ode on Eton College* Richardson, *Clarissa* T. Warton, *Pleasures of Melancholy*	British naval victories against France
1748	Thomson dies, *Castle of Indolence* published Cleland, *Memoirs of a Woman of Pleasure* Hume, *Philosophical Essays concerning Human Understanding* Smollett, *Roderick Random*	Peace of Aix-la-Chapelle
1749	Fielding, *Tom Jones* Johnson, *Vanity of Human Wishes*	

Year	Age	Life
1752	21	Visits Norfolk. Falls in love with cousin Theodora (died 1824), and she with him. Ashley Cowper's hopes for a better match eventually lead him to forbid their meeting (1755). Theodora never marries
1753	22	Enters Chambers in Middle Temple
1754	23	Called to the bar
1756	25	Writes five papers for Colman's *Connoisseur*
1757	26	Enters Inner Temple. Translates two satires of Horace
1759	28	Made Commissioner of Bankrupts, at £60 a year
1760–3	29–32	Inactive years in Inner Temple. Cowper reads, writes only occasionally and earns no money
1762	31	Translates Cantos *vi-viii* of Voltaire's *Henriade* for Smollett's edition

Year	Literary Context	Historical Events
1751	Sheridan born Fielding, *Amelia, Late Increase of Robbers* Gray, *Elegy* Smollett, *Peregrine Pickle*	Prince of Wales dies
1752	Chatterton born Lennox, *Female Quixote* Smart, *Poems on Several Occasions*	Clive takes Trichinopoloy
1753	Hogarth, *Analysis of Beauty* Richardson, *Sir Charles Grandison* Smollett, *Ferdinand Count Fathom*	
1754	Crabbe born Fielding dies	Pelham dies; Newcastle minstry. War against French in America
1755	Fielding, *Voyage to Lisbon* Johnson, *Dictionary*	Lisbon earthquake
1756	Godwin born	Seven Years War begins
1757	Blake born Burke, *Philosophical Enquiry into the Sublime and the Beautiful* Dyer, *The Fleece* Gray, *Odes*	Admiral Byng shot
1759	Burns born Mary Wollstonecraft born Collins dies	Fears of invasion
1760	Beckford born Goldsmith, *Chinese Letters* begun Sterne *Tristram Shandy* (i–ii) Smollett, *Sir Launcelot Greaves* (–1761)	George II dies. George III succeeds to the throne
1761	Churchill, *The Rosciad*	Pitt resigns
1762	Churchill, *The Ghost* (i–iii)	Bute ministry

Year	Age	Life
1763	32	Offered Clerkship of Journals of House of Lords by Ashley Cowper. The stress caused by the prospect of public examination brings about mental breakdown. Attempts at suicide. Brother removes him to Dr Cotton's asylum at St Albans
1763–5	32–4	At St Albans. Experiences evangelical-style conversion. Moves into lodgings in Huntingdon, and then to the home of the Revd Unwin
1766	35	Living with the Unwins. Begins to write a *Memoir*. Financed by friends, including Theodora and her sister Harriet, now Lady Hesketh. Takes up gardening
1767	36	Revd Unwin killed in riding accident. Moves with Mrs Unwin to Orchard Side, Olney where the ex-slave trader turned evangelical, John Newton, was curate
1770	39	Brother John Cowper dies, leaving a small legacy
1771	40	Encouraged by Newton, Cowper begins the *Olney Hymns*
1772	41	Becomes engaged to Mary Unwin
1773	42	Another breakdown occurs. Moves into Newton's vicarage, is treated by Dr Cotton, attempts suicide. The engagement is broken off

Year	Literary Context	Historical Events
1763	Shenstone dies Smart, *Song to David*	Peace of Paris. Wilkes publishes *North Briton* No. 45; arrested
1764	Radcliffe born Churchill dies: *The Candidate* published Hogarth dies Goldsmith, *The Traveller*	Wilkes barred from House of Commons
1765	Percy, *Reliques* Walpole, *Castle of Otranto*	Stamp Act taxes American colonies. Rockingham's ministry
1766	Anstey, *New Bath Guide* Goldsmith, *Vicar of Wakefield* Smollett, *Travels through France and Italy*	Stamp Act repealed. Chatham ministry
1767	Edgeworth born Jago, *Edge-Hill*	Grafton ministry
1768	Sterne dies Goldsmith, *The Good Natured Man* Gray, *Poems*	Wilkes sentenced for libel
1770	Akenside dies Chatterton dies Wordsworth born Burke, *Thoughts on the Present Discontents* Goldsmith, *The Deserted Village*	North ministry
1771	Gray dies Smart dies Smollett dies Scott born Mackenzie, *Man of Feeling* Smollett, *Humphrey Clinker*	Spain cedes the Falkland Islands to Britain
1772	Coleridge born	
1773	Goldsmith, *She Stoops to Conquer* Mackenzie, *Man of the World*	Boston 'tea party'

Year	Age	Life
1774	43	After a gradual recovery, Cowper moves back to Orchard Side. Takes in pet hares
1775–80	44–9	Living in seclusion at Olney
1779	48	*Olney Hymns* published
1780	49	Writes 'Verses on a Goldfinch', 'The Nightingale and Glow-worm'. Begins *Progress of Error* and *Truth*. Takes up sketching and carpentry
1781	50	*Anti-Thelyphthora* published anonymously. Completes *Table Talk* and *Expostulation*. Meets Lady Austen who would prompt the first book of *The Task*
1782	51	Publishes *Poems by William Cowper, of the Inner Temple, Esq.* Writes *John Gilpin*, published anonymously in the *Public Advertiser*. Writes *The Colubriad*
1783	52	*The Task* is begun

Year	Literary Context	Historical Events
1774	Goldsmith dies Southey born Chesterfield, *Letters to his Son* Kelly, *School for Wives*	First Congress of American colonies
1775	Austen born Burke, *Speech on Conciliation with the Colonies* Johnson, *Journey to the Western Islands of Scotland; Taxation no Tyranny* Sheridan, *The Rivals*	Battles of Lexington, Concord, and Bunker Hill
1776	Gibbon, *Decline and Fall of the Roman Empire* i (finished 1788) Smith, *Wealth of Nations*	American Declaration of Independence
1777	Chatterton, *Rowley Poems* Sheridan, *A Trip to Scarborough*	Burgoyne surrenders at Saratoga
1778	Hazlitt born Burney, *Evelina*	Pitt dies. France allies with America. Britain declares war on France
1779	Garrick dies Johnson, 'Lives' Sheridan, *The Critic*	Britain at war with Spain; siege of Gibraltar
1780	Crabbe, *The Candidate*	Gordon riots
1781	Crabbe, *The Library* Rousseau, *Confessions*	Cornwallis surrenders at Yorktown
1782	Burney, *Cecilia* Gilpin, *Observations on the River Wye*	
1783	Blake, *Poetical Sketches* Crabbe, *The Village*	Fox-North coalition. Pitt the Younger's Ministry. Peace of Versailles

Year	Age	Life
1784	53	*The Task* completed by October. *Tirocinium* written. Translating Homer. Friendship with Throckmortons of Weston Underwood
1785	54	*The Task* published by Joseph Johnson; warm critical response
1786	55	Moves to Weston Lodge. Publishes *Specimens* and *Proposals* for the Homer
1787	56	Cowper suffers another mental collapse
1788	57	Continues to live at Weston. Writes anti-slavery verses. Revising the *Iliad*: starts to translate the *Odyssey*
1790	59	Writes 'On the Receipt of my Mother's Picture'. Visited by his young cousin, John Johnson
1791	60	Homer published: Cowper receives £1000. Mrs Unwin struck with paralysis
1792	61	Mrs Unwin suffers second stroke. Abbott and Romney paint Cowper's portrait. Visits William Hayley at Eartham, Sussex
1793	62	Writes 'To Mary'. Mental health deteriorating

Year	Literary Context	Historical Events
1784	Johnson dies	India Act
1785	De Quincey born Peacock born Boswell, *Tour to the Hebrides*	
1786	Beckford, *Vathek* Burns, *Poems*	
1787	Wollstonecraft, *Thoughts on the Education of Daughters*	Warren Hastings impeached. Association for Abolition of Slave Trade formed. US Constitution signed
1788	Byron born Collins, *Ode on the Popular Superstitions of the Highlands*	Warren Hastings on trial. George III's 'madness'
1789	Blake, *Songs of Innocence* White, *Natural History of Selborne*	Bastille taken. Declaration of the Rights of Man
1790	Blake, *Marriage of Heaven and Hell* Burke, *Reflections on the French Revolution*	
1791	Boswell, *Life of Johnson*	French King escapes, but recaptured at Varennes
1792	Shelley born Wordsworth in France Gilpin, *Essays on Picturesque Beauty* Wollstonecraft, *Vindication of the Rights of Women*	Warren Hastings acquitted. Austria declares war on France
1793	Clare born Blake, *A Vision of the Daughters of Albion; America* Wordsworth, *Descriptive Sketches*	Louis XVI and Marie-Antoinette executed; the Terror; Marat murdered; Robespierre in power. France and Britain declare war

Year	Age	Life
1794	63	Final breakdown begins
1795	64	With Mrs Unwin and John Johnson, Cowper visits Mundesley in Norfolk
1796	65	At East Dereham. Mrs Unwin dies
1797–9	66–8	Remains at East Dereham, revising Homer
1799	68	Writes 'Montes Glaciales' and 'The Castaway'
1800	69	Translates some of Gay's *Fables*. Dies on 25 April. Buried East Dereham

Year	Literary Context	Historical Events
1794	Gibbon dies Blake, *Songs of Experience;* *Europe; Book of Urizen* Godwin, *Caleb Williams* Radcliffe, *The Mysteries of* *Udolpho*	Danton and Robespierre executed; Terror ends
1795	Boswell dies Keats born Blake, *Book of Los* Lewis, *Ambrosio, or The Monk*	Bonaparte in Italy. British troops evacuated from Continent
1796	Burns dies Burney, *Camilla* Coleridge, *Poems on Various* *Subjects*	
1797	Burke, Wollstonecraft and Walpole die Radcliffe, *The Italian*	Battles at Cape St Vincent and Camperdown
1798	Coleridge, *Fears in Solitude,* *France, an Ode,* and *Frost at* *Midnight* Wordsworth and Coleridge, *Lyrical Ballads*	Nelson defeats Bonaparte at Aboukir Bay
1799	Campbell, *The Pleasures of* *Hope*	
1800	Coleridge, *Poems* Edgeworth, *Castle Rackrent*	Battles of Alexandria, Hohenlinden, Marengo

Introduction

When Marianne Dashwood (*Sense and Sensibility*) insists that to read Cowper without animation is the stigma of a dull soul, one wonders whether Jane Austen was not scoring a cheap shot at the expense of her heroine's tender, if rhapsodic, affections. In fact, there are frequent invitations in Cowper's poetry to indulge those fine feelings for which Marianne voiced such enthusiasm. Moreover, in *Mansfield Park*, when Fanny Price (surely a spirit of approved temperance) quietly laments the scars that proceed from landscape 'improvement', she is allowed to summon Cowper as a witness: 'Ye fallen avenues, once more I mourn your fate unmerited' (*The Task*, I, 338–9). The lines refer to one of Cowper's favoured walks at Weston Underwood, but Fanny could have quoted, with equal or greater effect, from 'The Poplar Field' where Cowper plays upon the same elegiac refrain of nostalgia and loss.

Early reviewers had applauded Cowper for his humanity and his sentiment, and drew attention to the freshness of his emotional landscapes. They were responding to a new world of feeling – by turns affectionate, melancholic, enthusiastic, and always personal. Such qualities in the man (two biographies had been published in 1803), and in the poetry, go some way to explaining his attraction for Austen. There was much that she might admire in his conservatism. There was a steadiness in Cowper's descriptions of pious and civilised domesticity, and a wisdom in his moral opposition to fashionable existence in the metropolis. At the same time, there was an insistence on the 'heart's' affections having a currency equal to the 'head's' good sense. Cowper's cameos of rural life are touched by a tenderness and imaginativce warmth that frequently borders on the sentimental. When Marianne bids a tearful adieu to the trees surrounding her home at Norland, she could be imagined clutching a volume of Cowper's verse to her breast. The scene is recorded in silence by Austen, partly to point up the comedy of Marianne's effusiveness, but also perhaps because Austen read from the same book.

Historically, Cowper occupies the ground that the Augustan writers had given up to the 'age of sensibility'. By education and temperament he was faithful to tradition, and, in many ways, acknowledges his literary inheritance, even when modifying it. However, the character of his poetry, which sustained his popularity after the publication of *The Task* (1785), was, above all, the richness of its emotional colouring. Cowper never lost his instinct for moral and doctrinal instruction, but he was also sympathetic to the growing conviction that the reader should be brought to *feel* what was right rather than simply be argued into submission. In the late eighteenth century ideas such as these stood in at the birth of the new 'man (and woman) of feeling'. They also began to influence the ways in which readers were expected to respond to, or 'appreciate' poetry: and Cowper, himself, declared for the age when he wrote to Mary Unwin's son in 1782: 'persons of much sensibility are always persons of taste; a taste for poetry depends indeed upon that very article more than upon any other'.

The 'tender sentiment' for which Cowper was justly famous is often associated with the broadly humanitarian impact of his co-religionists in the Methodist movement. It receives its most obvious expression in the four 'anti-slavery' poems of 1788. They were taken up enthusiastically by the abolitionists, although, as poetry, it might be argued that they suffered from being too precisely tailored to a radical agenda. These poems, together with a 'Sonnet to William Wilberforce, Esq.', are the voice of public conscience, but they are also part of an insistent cadence of indignation in the face of inhumanity that echoes through the fabric of the work. Cowper opens the second book of *The Task* (1–47), for instance, with a broadside against racist oppression that clearly has British imperial policy in its sights. He perceives a depth of prejudice that runs deeper than mere profiteering:

> [Man] finds his fellow guilty of a skin
> Not colour'd like his own.

Cowper is sensitive to the hypocrisy that legally frees a slave fortunate enough to step on British soil, yet endorses the trade. He is also specifically critical of the mercantile greed that fuelled the expansion of empire:

> Is India free? and does she wear her plum'd
> And jewell'd turban with a smile of peace.
> Or do we grind her still?
> (*The Task, IV*, 28–30)

Although it should be noted that he was somewhat less sympathetic to the colonies in North America. Perhaps worst of all, as Cowper laments to John Newton, himself a one-time slaver, the perpetrators of these barbarities describe themselves as Christians (letter of 30 October 1784). Less brutal, but in some ways more poignant, is the tale of Omai, the South Sea Islander (*The Task*, I, 620–77), who was brought to England in one of Captain Cook's ships, lionised, presented to George III, and eventually returned to his native Tahiti. Cowper treats the 'gentle savage' with sympathy, but it is immediately noticeable that he has no interest in subscribing to the growing vogue for the 'noble savage'. In fact, his comments on 'the favour'd isles . . . plac'd remote/From all that science traces, art invents/Or inspiration teaches' suggest that Cowper is more than a little sceptical regarding the claims of romantic primitivism (see also the gypsies of Book I, 557–91). Omai's ignorant simplicity is used to highlight the glittering soullessness of European civilisation, which in turn infects him with a sad dissatisfaction when he is returned, a victim of fashionable whim, to his 'homestall thatch'd with leaves'. Cowper uses his story as an exemplum and the coda is of a piece with his general observations on imperial exploitation:

> We found no bait
> To tempt us in thy country. Doing good,
> Disinterested good, is not our trade.

It is a moral fable, but the solitary figure of Omai, gazing out to sea in hopes of spotting a British sail, is coloured by Cowper's sensitivity to the Tahitian's suffering. As he wrote to John Newton on 6 October 1783: 'We brought away an Indian, and having debauched him, we sent him home again to communicate the infection to his country; fine sport to be sure, but such as will not defray the cost.'

Cowper's voice of protest is a blend of the theological and the political. It varies from the intonations of biblical prophecy to the scathing irony of an outraged citizen. In the third book of *The Task* (290–351) Cowper offers an eloquent and painful vision of a countryside defiled by the pitiless cruelty of man's addiction to bloodsports. It is both a desecration and an offence against humanity's supposedly rational nature:

> Detested sport,
> That owes its pleasure to another's pain;
> That feeds upon the sobs and dying shrieks
> Of harmless nature . . .

It was this capacity for sympathy that most put Cowper in touch with the temper of the times. It is especially apparent in his treatment of the animal kingdom. Here, if anywhere, he is vulnerable to accusations of sentimentality, and a simple checklist of titles might suggest a hint of whimsy: 'On a Spaniel Called Beau', 'The Retired Cat', 'Epitaph on a Hare', 'On the Death of Mrs Throckmorton's Bulfinch', etc. It is rare, however, for these poems to lapse into the mawkish or coy. They are pieces that often provide a revealing biographical dimension, which Cowper surely legitimises by the way that he draws attention to himself in the poetry. Sometimes, in a manner reminiscent of Thomas Gray, the verses are buoyed up by an attractive self-mockery. In his poem to the spaniel Beau, a slightly self-righteous Cowper takes the animal to task for murdering birds. The dog cites nature in his defence, and concludes with a tart observation on what may be Cowper's own preoccupation with his ineffectual life in retreat. The poet seen from below:

> If killing birds be such a crime,
> (Which I can hardly see)
> What think you, Sir, of killing Time
> With verse address'd to me?

'The Retired Cat' is another such, where the poet's cat, luxuriating in the warm, womblike comfort of a linen-filled drawer, is shut in and forgotten. The melancholy panic that ensues when she finds herself incarcerated and unmissed again suggests Cowper's wry contemplation of his own reflection. The keeping of pets, together with such gentlemanly pursuits as gardening, sketching and carpentry, had filled Cowper's days with a necessary therapy: especially when what he called the 'unambiguous footsteps of God' became too insistent. Here was a kingdom over which he could exercise some control, and his involvement in daily tasks lent a stability to his life. The 'Epitaph on a Hare', in memory of 'Old Tiney', has charm in its accuracy of observation and genuine pathos as it recalls Cowper's emotional dependency upon the animal:

> I kept him for his humour's sake
> For oft he would beguile
> My heart of thoughts that made it ache,
> And force me to a smile.

Even the bizarre story of Mrs Throckmorton's bullfinch may be touched by shadows from the poet's life. On the surface, it is a lightweight, mock-heroic account of the bird's death beneath the teeth of a foraging rat: the sole memento is 'Bully's beak'. Yet the caged hysteria of the screaming bird as it watches the rat stripping away its wooden protection leaves a strangely disturbing emotional residue.

The poems that open this volume speak even more directly of the poet's anxious obsessions. They are glimpses into what might be described as Cowper's 'dark night of the soul', moments when he was overcome by the conviction that God had singled him out for a particular damnation. Images of storm, shipwreck, isolation crowd in upon one another, as they articulate Cowper's horrified feelings of being overwhelmed. The most dramatic instance is Cowper's last poem 'The Castaway' (1799). The narrative is taken from Richard Walter's *A Voyage Round the World by George Anson* (1748) which describes how a sailor, swept overboard, is left to drown as the ship is unable to put about. Gradually his cries for help fade on the ear until they are unheard by his comrades:

> For then, by toil subdued, he drank
> The stifling wave, and then he sank.

The episode becomes fraught with desperate images of alienation, loneliness and exhausted terror as Cowper pictures himself engulfed and rejected:

> But I, beneath a rougher sea,
> And whelm'd in deeper gulphs than he.

The emotional fabric of the poem is intensely painful. Three years earlier he had written to his cousin, Lady Hesketh: 'One thing and only one is left me, the wish that I had never existed' (30 May 1796). Exactly one month after the final date on the manuscript of the poem Cowper was dead.

The abandoned sailor, the marooned Selkirk, even the 800 souls that were sucked into the depths aboard the *Royal George*, all of them, in Cowper's imagination, act out the drama of his spiritual despair. In poems like these, sometimes directly, sometimes obliquely, the poet witnesses to his personal suffering and relies upon the reader's willingness to engage with that experience. In exposing his feelings in the way that he does, Cowper offers a guarantee of sincerity, a virtue soon to be held in esteem by Romantic writers. On occasion, the utterances will be painful, but there will be no attempt to mediate them through an elegant rhetoric. To speak from the heart is to speak simply. When Cowper turns to Mary Unwin (and by extension, to the reader) in the first book of *The Task* (150–2), he makes a declaration that could not help but attract Wordsworth as he sought to justify his poetry in the Preface to the *Lyrical Ballads* (1800):

> Thou know'st my praise of nature most sincere,
> And that my raptures are not conjur'd up
> To serve occasions of poetic pomp,
> But genuine . . .

The intensity of poems like 'The Castaway' is largely absent from *The Task*. Such a generalisation demands immediate qualification, of course, because Cowper's most famous lines upon his tortured spirit appear in the third book of that poem (108–16):

> I was a stricken deer, that left the herd
> Long since; with many an arrow deep infixt
> My panting side was charg'd when I withdrew
> To seek a tranquil death in distant shades.
> There was I found by one who had himself
> Been hurt by th' archers.

On this occasion, there is salvation. Cowper's merging of his own pain with Christ's suffering brings about a healing. There is, here, a conventional expression of spiritual rehabilitation which is not to be found in the shorter and more disturbing poems. Furthermore, as the passage progresses, the intimacy of the opening scene fades. Cowper describes life in retirement with a few chosen friends, and then in the lines that follow (124–90), there is a perceptible shift from the private to the public, as Cowper peeps through his 'loopholes of retreat' (IV, 88), and laments the 'delusions' and 'fancied happiness' of the world at large. The final section launches into a wonderfully fundamentalist diatribe against the sinful impertinence of modern science. This is Cowper in full prophetic flow, anticipating in his tone the outcry that would meet Darwin when he published *Origin of Species* some eighty years later. In little more than sixty lines, Cowper has moved from a personal and poignant expression of spiritual vulnerability to a Methodist version of himself as oracle of doom.

The Task was, in many of its aspects, a very conventional work. It is a long, discursive poem in blank verse, which moves digressively from topic to topic, observing, reflecting, speculating. At the centre is the English countryside as an image of permanence – a cohesive metaphor drawing all the narratives and meditations and descriptions into a loose relationship. It was a poem with many antecedents. Behind *The Task* lie poems such as Denham's *Cooper's Hill* (1642), Philips's *Cyder* (1708), Pope's *Windsor Forest* (1713), Dyer's *The Fleece* (1757) and, most of all, Thomson's *The Seasons* (1730).

Most of these works had as part of their agenda the discovery, in verse, of a sense of national identity. To this end, the countryside was often asssertively politicised, and frequently cast in the mould of a new, commercially driven Golden Age. It is here, especially, that Cowper parts company. Historically, he is an interesting barometer of changing sensibilities. The passage from Book III (150–90) is a measure of just how far Cowper distances himself from the optimistic visions of Newtonian science. Both his temperament and his religion told him that he inhabited 'a shatter'd world' where the best hope for a nation lay in private piety.

Cowper has little sympathy with the aggressive, mercantile imperialism that tainted so many of the earlier poets' landscapes. The quietism of rural retirement was his own answer, and what he offered was arguably original. It was a sensitive evocation of his own daily existence which assumed that his personal feelings and his response to natural beauty would be of interest to the reader.

MICHAEL BRUCE

William Cowper

Lines Written During
a Period of Insanity

Hatred and vengeance, my eternal portion,
Scarce can endure delay of execution,
Wait, with impatient readiness, to seize my
                                        Soul in a moment.

Damn'd below Judas: more abhorr'd than he was,
Who for a few pence sold his holy Master.
Twice betrayed Jesus me, the last delinquent,
                                        Deems the profanest.

Man disavows, and Deity disowns me:
Hell might afford my miseries a shelter;
Therefore hell keeps her ever hungry mouths all
                                        Bolted against me.

Hard lot! encompass'd with a thousand dangers;
Weary, faint, trembling with a thousand terrors;
I'm called, if vanquish'd, to receive a sentence
                                        Worse than Abiram's.

Him the vindictive rod of angry justice
Sent quick and howling to the centre headlong;
I, fed with judgment, in a fleshly tomb, am
                                        Buried above ground.

The Castaway

Obscurest night involv'd the sky,
   Th' Atlantic billows roar'd,
When such a destin'd wretch as I,
   Wash'd headlong from on board,
Of friends, of hope, of all bereft,
His floating home for ever left.

No braver chief could Albion boast
   Than he, with whom he went,
Nor ever ship left Albion's coast
   With warmer wishes sent.   10
He lov'd them both, but both in vain,
Nor him beheld, nor her again.

Not long beneath the whelming brine,
   Expert to swim, he lay,
Nor soon he felt his strength decline,
   Or courage die away;
But wag'd with death a lasting strife,
Supported by despair of life.

He shouted: nor his friends had fail'd
   To check the vessel's course,   20
But so the furious blast prevail'd,
   That, pitiless perforce,
They left their outcast mate behind,
And scudded still before the wind.

Some succour yet they could afford,
   And, such as storms allow,
The cask, the coop, the floated cord,
   Delay'd not to bestow.
But he (they knew) nor ship nor shore,
Whate'er they gave, should visit more.   30

Nor, cruel as it seem'd, could he
   Their haste himself condemn,

Aware that flight, in such a sea,
    Alone could rescue them;
Yet bitter felt it still to die
Deserted, and his friends so nigh.

He long survives, who lives an hour
    In ocean, self-upheld;
And so long he, with unspent pow'r,
    His destiny repell'd;   40
And ever, as the minutes flew,
Entreated help, or cried – 'Adieu!'

At length, his transient respite past,
    His comrades, who before
Had heard his voice in ev'ry blast,
    Could catch the sound no more:
For then, by toil subdued, he drank
The stifling wave, and then he sank.

No poet wept him: but the page
    Of narrative sincere,   50
That tells his name, his worth, his age,
    Is wet with Anson's tear:
And tears by bards or heroes shed
Alike immortalize the dead.

I therefore purpose not, or dream,
    Descanting on his fate,
To give the melancholy theme
    A more enduring date:
But misery still delights to trace
Its semblance in another's case.   60

No voice divine the storm allay'd,
    No light propitious shone,
When, snatch'd from all effectual aid,
    We perish'd, each, alone:
But I, beneath a rougher sea,
And whelm'd in deeper gulfs than he.

Verses,

Supposed to be written by Alexander Selkirk, during his
solitary abode in the island of Juan Fernandez

I am monarch of all I survey,
    My right there is none to dispute;
From the centre all round to the sea,
    I am lord of the fowl and the brute.
O solitude! where are the charms
    That sages have seen in thy face?
Better dwell in the midst of alarms,
    Than reign in this horrible place.

I am out of humanity's reach,
    I must finish my journey alone,
Never hear the sweet music of speech;
    I start at the sound of my own.
The beasts that roam over the plain,
    My form with indifference see;
They are so unacquainted with man,
    Their tameness is shocking to me.

Society, friendship, and love,
    Divinely bestowed upon man,
Oh had I the wings of a dove,
    How soon would I taste you again!
My sorrows I then might assuage
    In the ways of religion and truth,
Might learn from the wisdom of age,
    And be cheer'd by the sallies of youth.

Religion! what treasure untold
    Resides in that heavenly word!
More precious than silver and gold,

Or all that this earth can afford.
But the sound of the church-going bell
   These valleys and rocks never heard,
Ne'er sigh'd at the sound of a knell,
    Or smil'd when a sabbath appear'd.

Ye winds, that have made me your sport,
   Convey to this desolate shore
Some cordial endearing report
   Of a land I shall visit no more.
My friends, do they now and then send
   A wish or a thought after me?
O tell me I yet have a friend,
   Though a friend I am never to see.

How fleet is a glance of the mind!
   Compar'd with the speed of its flight,
The tempest itself lags behind,
   And the swift-wing'd arrows of light.
When I think of my own native land,
   In a moment I seem to be there;
But alas! recollection at hand
   Soon hurries me back to despair.

But the sea-fowl is gone to her nest,
   The beast is laid down in his lair,
Even here is a season of rest,
   And I to my cabin repair.
There is mercy in ev'ry place,
   And mercy, encouraging thought!
Gives even affliction a grace,
   And reconciles man to his lot.

On the Loss of the Royal George

Written when the news arrived

Toll for the brave –
  The brave! that are no more:
All sunk beneath the wave,
  Fast by their native shore.
Eight hundred of the brave,
  Whose courage well was tried,
Had made the vessel heel,
  And laid her on her side;
A land-breeze shook the shrouds,
  And she was overset;
Down went the Royal George,
  With all her crew complete.

Toll for the brave –
  Brave Kempenfelt is gone,
His last sea fight is fought,
  His work of glory done.
It was not in the battle,
  No tempest gave the shock,
She sprang no fatal leak,
  She ran upon no rock;
His sword was in its sheath,
  His fingers held the pen,
When Kempenfelt went down,
  With twice four hundred men.

Weigh the vessel up,
  Once dreaded by our foes,
And mingle with our cup
  The tears that England owes.
Her timbers yet are sound,
  And she may float again,
Full charg'd with England's thunder,
  And plough the distant main –
But Kempenfelt is gone,

His victories are o'er;
  And he and his eight hundred
    Shall plough the wave no more.

The Shrubbery

Written in a time of affliction

Oh happy shades! to me unblest,
  Friendly to peace, but not to me,
How ill the scene that offers rest,
  And heart that cannot rest, agree!

This glassy stream, that spreading pine,
  Those alders quiv'ring to the breeze,
Might sooth a soul less hurt than mine,
  And please, if any thing could please.

But fix'd unalterable care
  Foregoes not what she feels within,
Shows the same sadness ev'ry where,
  And slights the season and the scene.

For all that pleas'd in wood or lawn,
  While peace possess'd these silent bow'rs,
Her animating smile withdrawn,
  Has lost its beauties and its pow'rs.

The saint or moralist should tread
  This moss-grown alley, musing slow;
They seek, like me, the secret shade,
  But not, like me, to nourish woe.

Me fruitful scenes and prospects waste,
  Alike admonish not to roam;
These tell me of enjoyments past,
  And those of sorrows yet to come.

Yardley Oak

Survivor sole, and hardly such, of all
That once lived here, thy brethren, at my birth
(Since which I number threescore winters past),
A shatter'd veteran, hollow-trunk'd perhaps
As now, and with excoriate forks deform,
Relicts of ages! Could a mind, imbued
With truth from heav'n, created thing adore,
I might with rev'rence kneel, and worship thee.

It seems idolatry, with some excuse,
When our forefather Druids in their oaks   10
Imagin'd sanctity. The conscience, yet
Unpurified by an authentic act
Of amnesty, the meed of blood divine,
Lov'd not the light, but, gloomy, into gloom
Of thickest shades, like Adam after taste
Of fruit proscrib'd, as to a refuge, fled.

Thou wast a bauble once; a cup and ball,
Which babes might play with; and the thievish jay,
Seeking her food, with ease might have purloin'd
The auburn nut that held thee, swallowing down   20
Thy yet close-folded latitude of boughs
And all thine embryo vastness, at a gulp.
But Fate thy growth decreed: autumnal rains
Beneath thy parent tree mellow'd the soil
Design'd thy cradle, and a skipping deer,
With pointed hoof dibbling the glebe, prepar'd
The soft receptacle, in which, secure,
Thy rudiments should sleep the winter through.

So Fancy dreams. Disprove it, if ye can,
Ye reas'ners broad awake, whose busy searce   30
Of argument, employ'd too oft amiss,
Sifts half the pleasures of short life away.

Thou fell'st mature, and in the loamy clod
Swelling with vegetative force instinct
Didst burst thine egg, as theirs the fabled Twins,
Now stars; two lobes, protruding, pair'd exact;
A leaf succeeded, and another leaf,

And, all the elements thy puny growth
Fost'ring propitious, thou becam'st a twig.
   Who liv'd when thou wast such? Oh couldst thou speak,   40
As in Dodona once thy kindred trees
Oracular, I would not curious ask
The future, best unknown, but at thy mouth
Inquisitive, the less ambiguous past.
   By thee I might correct, erroneous oft,
The clock of history, facts and events
Timing more punctual, unrecorded facts
Recov'ring, and misstated setting right –
Desp'rate attempt, till trees shall speak again!
   Time made thee what thou wast – king of the woods;   50
And Time hath made thee what thou art – a cave
For owls to roost in. Once thy spreading boughs
O'erhung the champain; and the numerous flock,
That graz'd it, stood beneath that ample cope
Uncrowded, yet safe-shelter'd from the storm.
No flock frequents thee now. Thou hast outliv'd
Thy popularity, and art become
(Unless verse rescue thee awhile) a thing
Forgotten, as the foliage of thy youth.
   While thus through all the stages thou hast push'd   60
Of treeship – first a seedling, hid in grass;
Then twig; then sapling; and, as century roll'd
Slow after century, a giant-bulk
Of girth enormous, with moss-cushion'd root
Upheav'd above the soil, and sides emboss'd
With prominent wens globose, till at the last
The rottenness, which time is charg'd to inflict
On other mighty ones, found also thee.
   What exhibitions various hath the world
Witness'd of mutability in all   70
That we account most durable below!
Change is the diet, on which all subsist,
Created changeable, and change at last
Destroys them. Skies uncertain now the heat
Transmitting cloudless, and the solar beam
Now quenching in a boundless sea of clouds –
Calm and alternate storm, moisture and drought,

Invigorate by turns the springs of life
In all that live, plant, animal, and man,
And in conclusion mar them. Nature's threads,   80
Fine passing thought, e'en in her coarsest works,
Delight in agitation, yet sustain,
The force, that agitates, not unimpair'd,
But, worn by frequent impulse, to the cause
Of their best tone their dissolution owe.

Thought cannot spend itself, comparing still
The great and little of thy lot, thy growth
From almost nullity into a state
Of matchless grandeur, and declension thence,
Slow, into such magnificent decay.   90
Time was, when, settling on thy leaf, a fly
Could shake thee to the root – and time has been
When tempests could not. At thy firmest age
Thou hadst within thy bole solid contents,
That might have ribb'd the sides and plank'd the deck
Of some flagg'd admiral; and tortuous arms,
The shipwright's darling treasure, didst present
To the four-quarter'd winds, robust and bold,
Warp'd into tough knee-timber, many a load.
But the axe spar'd thee. In those thriftier days   100
Oaks fell not, hewn by thousands, to supply
The bottomless demands of contest, wag'd
For senatorial honours. Thus to Time
The task was left to whittle thee away
With his sly scythe, whose ever-nibbling edge,
Noiseless, an atom and an atom more
Disjoining from the rest, has, unobserved,
Achieved a labour, which had, far and wide,
By man perform'd, made all the forest ring.

Embowell'd now, and of thy ancient self   110
Possessing nought but the scoop'd rind, that seems
An huge throat, calling to the clouds for drink,
Which it would give in riv'lets to thy root,
Thou temptest none, but rather much forbid'st
The feller's toil, which thou couldst ill requite.
Yet is thy root sincere, sound as the rock,
A quarry of stout spurs, and knotted fangs,

Which, crook'd into a thousand whimsies, clasp
The stubborn soil, and hold thee still erect.
  So stands a kingdom, whose foundations yet   120
Fail not, in virtue and in wisdom laid,
Though all the superstructure, by the tooth
Pulveriz'd of venality, a shell
Stands now, and semblance only of itself.
  Thine arms have left thee. Winds have rent them off
Long since, and rovers of the forest wild
With bow and shaft, have burnt them. Some have left
A splinter'd stump, bleach'd to a snowy white;
And some, memorial none, where once they grew.
Yet life still lingers in thee, and puts forth   130
Proof not contemptible of what she can,
Even where death predominates. The spring
Finds thee not less alive to her sweet force
Than yonder upstarts of the neighbouring wood,
So much thy juniors, who their birth receiv'd
Half a millennium since the date of thine.
  But since, although well qualified by age
To teach, no spirit dwells in thee, nor voice
May be expected from thee, seated here
On thy distorted root, with hearers none   140
Or prompter, save the scene, I will perform
Myself the oracle, and will discourse
In my own ear such matter as I may.
Thou, like myself, hast stage by stage attain'd
Life's wintry bourn; thou, after many years,
I after few; but few or many prove
A span in retrospect; for I can touch
With my least finger's end my own decease
And with extended thumb my natal hour,
And hadst thou also skill in measurement   150
As I, the past would seem as short to thee.
Evil and few – said Jacob – at an age
Thrice mine, and few and evil, I may think
The Prediluvian race, whose buxom youth
Endured two centuries, accounted theirs.
'Shortliv'd as foliage is the race of man.
The wind shakes down the leaves, the budding grove

Soon teems with others, and in spring they grow.
So pass mankind. One generation meets
Its destin'd period, and a new succeeds.'   160
Such was the tender but undue complaint
Of the Mæonian in old time; for who
Would drawl out centuries in tedious strife
Severe with mental and corporeal ill
And would not rather chuse a shorter race
To glory, a few decads here below?
  One man alone, the Father of us all,
Drew not his life from woman; never gaz'd,
With mute unconsciousness of what he saw,
On all around him; learn'd not by degrees,   170
Nor owed articulation to his ear;
But, moulded by his Maker into Man
At once, upstood intelligent, survey'd
All creatures, with precision understood
Their purport, uses, properties, assign'd
To each his name significant, and fill'd
With love and wisdom, render'd back to heaven
In praise harmonious the first air he drew.
He was excus'd the penalties of dull
Minority. No tutor charg'd his hand   180
With the thought-tracing quill, or task'd his mind
With problems. History, not wanted yet,
Lean'd on her elbow, watching Time, whose course,
Eventful, should supply her with a theme;

*   *   *   *   *   *   *   *

The Poplar Field

The poplars are fell'd, farewell to the shade
And the whispering sound of the cool colonnade,
The winds play no longer, and sing in the leaves,
Nor Ouse on his bosom their image receives.

Twelve years have elaps'd since I last took a view
Of my favourite field, and the bank where they grew;

And now in the grass behold they are laid,
And the tree is my seat that once lent me a shade.

The blackbird has fled to another retreat,
Where the hazels afford him a screen from the heat,
And the scene where his melody charm'd me before,
Resounds with his sweet-flowing ditty no more.

My fugitive years are all hasting away,
And I must ere long lie as lowly as they,
With a turf on my breast, and a stone at my head,
Ere another such grove shall rise in its stead.

'Tis a sight to engage me, if any thing can,
To muse on the perishing pleasures of man;
Though his life be a dream, his enjoyments, I see,
Have a being less durable even than he.

The Diverting History of John Gilpin,

Showing how he went farther than he intended,
and came safe home again

John Gilpin was a citizen
  Of credit and renown,
A train-band captain eke was he
  Of famous London town.

John Gilpin's spouse said to her dear,
  – Though wedded we have been
These twice ten tedious years, yet we
  No holiday have seen.

To-morrow is our wedding-day,
  And we will then repair

Unto the Bell at Edmonton,
   All in a chaise and pair.

My sister and my sister's child,
   Myself, and children three,
Will fill the chaise; so you must ride
   On horseback after we.

He soon replied – I do admire
   Of womankind but one,
And you are she, my dearest dear,
   Therefore it shall be done.   20

I am a linen-draper bold,
   As all the world doth know,
And my good friend the calender
   Will lend his horse to go.

Quoth Mrs Gilpin – That's well said;
   And, for that wine is dear,
We will be furnish'd with our own,
   Which is both bright and clear.

John Gilpin kiss'd his loving wife;
   O'erjoyed was he to find   30
That, though on pleasure she was bent,
   She had a frugal mind.

The morning came, the chaise was brought,
   But yet was not allow'd
To drive up to the door, lest all
   Should say that she was proud.

So three doors off the chaise was stay'd,
   Where they did all get in,
Six precious souls, and all agog
   To dash through thick and thin!   40

Smack went the whip, round went the wheels,
   Were never folk so glad,

The stones did rattle underneath,
    As if Cheapside were mad.

John Gilpin at his horse's side
    Seized fast the flowing mane,
And up he got, in haste to ride,
    But soon came down again.

For saddle-tree scarce reach'd had he,
    His journey to begin,   50
When, turning round his head, he saw
    Three customers come in.

So down he came; for loss of time,
    Although it griev'd him sore,
Yet loss of pence, full well he knew,
    Would trouble him much more.

'Twas long before the customers
    Were suited to their mind,
When Betty screaming came down stairs,
    'The wine is left behind!'   60

Good lack! quoth he – yet bring it me,
    My leathern belt likewise,
In which I bear my trusty sword
    When I do exercise.

Now Mistress Gilpin, careful soul,
    Had two stone bottles found,
To hold the liquor that she lov'd,
    And keep it safe and sound.

Each bottle had a curling ear,
    Through which the belt he drew,   70
And hung a bottle on each side
    To make his balance true.

Then, over all, that he might be
    Equipp'd from top to toe,

His long red cloak, well brush'd and neat
   He manfully did throw.

Now see him mounted once again
   Upon his nimble steed,
Full slowly pacing o'er the stones,
   With caution and good heed.   80

But finding soon a smoother road
   Beneath his well-shod feet,
The snorting beast began to trot,
   Which gall'd him in his seat.

So, Fair and softly, John he cried,
   But John he cried in vain;
That trot became a gallop soon,
   In spite of curb and rein.

So stooping down, as needs he must
   Who cannot sit upright,   90
He grasp'd the mane with both his hands,
   And eke with all his might.

His horse, who never in that sort
   Had handled been before,
What thing upon his back had got
   Did wonder more and more.

Away went Gilpin neck or nought,
   Away went hat and wig!
He little dreamt, when he set out,
   Of running such a rig!   100

The wind did blow, the cloak did fly,
   Like streamer long and gay,
Till, loop and button failing both,
   At last it flew away.

Then might all people well discern
   The bottles he had slung;

A bottle swinging at each side
   As hath been said or sung.

The dogs did bark, the children scream'd,
   Up flew the windows all;
And every soul cried out – Well done!
   As loud as he could bawl.

110

Away went Gilpin – who but he?
   His fame soon spread around –
He carries weight! he rides a race!
   'Tis for a thousand pound.

And still as fast as he drew near,
   'Twas wonderful to view
How in a trice the turnpike-men
   Their gates wide open threw.

120

And now as he went bowing down
   His reeking head full low,
The bottles twain behind his back
   Were shatter'd at a blow.

Down ran the wine into the road,
   Most piteous to be seen,
Which made his horse's flanks to smoke
   As they had basted been.

But still he seem'd to carry weight,
   With leathern girdle brac'd;
For all might see the bottle-necks
   Still dangling at his waist.

130

Thus all through merry Islington
   These gambols he did play,
And till he came unto the Wash
   Of Edmonton so gay.

And there he threw the wash about
   On both sides of the way,

Just like unto a trundling mop,
    Or a wild goose at play.   140

At Edmonton his loving wife
    From the balcony spied
Her tender husband, wond'ring much
    To see how he did ride.

Stop, stop, John Gilpin! – Here's the house –
    They all at once did cry;
The dinner waits and we are tir'd:
    Said Gilpin – so am I!

But yet his horse was not a whit
    Inclin'd to tarry there,   150
For why? his owner had a house
    Full ten miles off, at Ware.

So like an arrow swift he flew
    Shot by an archer strong;
So did he fly – which brings me to
    The middle of my song.

Away went Gilpin, out of breath,
    And sore against his will,
Till at his friend's the calender's
    His horse at last stood still.   160

The calender amaz'd to see
    His neighbour in such trim,
Laid down his pipe, flew to the gate,
    And thus accosted him –

What news? what news? your tidings tell,
    Tell me you must and shall –
Say why bare-headed you are come,
    Or why you come at all?

Now Gilpin had a pleasant wit,
    And lov'd a timely joke,   170

And thus unto the calender
  In merry guise he spoke –

I came because your horse would come;
  And, if I well forebode,
My hat and wig will soon be here,
  They are upon the road.

The calender, right glad to find
  His friend in merry pin,
Return'd him not a single word,
  But to the house went in;   180

Whence straight he came with hat and wig;
  A wig that flow'd behind,
A hat not much the worse for wear,
  Each comely in its kind.

He held them up and in his turn
  Thus show'd his ready wit –
My head is twice as big as yours,
  They therefore needs must fit.

But let me scrape the dirt away
  That hangs upon your face;   190
And stop and eat, for well you may
  Be in a hungry case.

Said John – It is my wedding-day,
  And all the world would stare,
If wife should dine at Edmonton
  And I should dine at Ware!

So, turning to his horse, he said –
  I am in haste to dine,
'Twas for your pleasure you came here,
  You shall go back for mine.   200

Ah, luckless speech, and bootless boast!
  For which he paid full dear;

For while he spake a braying ass
    Did sing most loud and clear.

Whereat his horse did snort, as he
    Had heard a lion roar,
And gallop'd off with all his might,
    As he had done before.

Away went Gilpin, and away
    Went Gilpin's hat and wig;   210
He lost them sooner than at first –
    For why? They were too big!

Now mistress Gilpin, when she saw
    Her husband posting down
Into the country far away,
    She pull'd out half a crown;

And thus unto the youth she said
    That drove them to the Bell –
This shall be yours when you bring back
    My husband safe and well.   220

The youth did ride, and soon did meet
    John coming back amain;
Whom in a trice he tried to stop
    By catching at his rein.

But, not performing what he meant,
    And gladly would have done,
The frighted steed he frighted more,
    And made him faster run.

Away went Gilpin, and away
    Went post-boy at his heels! –   230
The post-boy's horse right glad to miss
    The lumbering of the wheels.

Six gentlemen upon the road,
    Thus seeing Gilpin fly,

With post-boy scamp'ring in the rear,
  They raised the hue and cry.

Stop thief, stop thief – a highwayman!
  Not one of them was mute;
And all and each that pass'd that way
  Did join in the pursuit.   240

And now the turnpike gates again
  Flew open in short space,
The toll-man thinking as before
  That Gilpin rode a race.

And so he did – and won it too! –
  For he got first to town,
Nor stopp'd till where he had got up
  He did again get down.

Now let us sing – Long live the king,
  And Gilpin long live he;   250
And when he next doth ride abroad,
  May I be there to see!

The Colubriad

Close by the threshold of a door nail'd fast
Three kittens sat: each kitten look'd aghast.
I, passing swift and inattentive by,
At the three kittens cast a careless eye;
Not much concern'd to know what they did there,
Not deeming kittens worth a poet's care.
But presently a loud and furious hiss
Caused me to stop and to exclaim – What's this?
When, lo! upon the threshold met my view,
With head erect, and eyes of fiery hue,   10
A viper, long as Count de Grasse's queue.
Forth from his head his forked tongue he throws,

Darting it full against a kitten's nose;
Who having never seen in field or house
The like, sat still and silent, as a mouse:
Only, projecting with attention due
Her whisker'd face, she ask'd him – Who are you?
On to the hall went I, with pace not slow,
But swift as lightning, for a long Dutch hoe;
With which well arm'd I hasten'd to the spot,   20
To find the viper. But I found him not;
And, turning up the leaves and shrubs around,
Found only, that he was not to be found.
But still the kittens, sitting as before,
Sat watching close the bottom of the door.
I hope – said I – the villain I would kill
Has slipp'd between the door and the door's sill;
And if I make despatch and follow hard,
No doubt but I shall find him in the yard –
For long ere now it should have been rehears'd,   30
'Twas in the garden that I found him first.
E'en there I found him; there the full-grown cat
His head, with velvet paw did gently pat,
As curious as the kittens erst had been
To learn what this phenomenon might mean.
Fill'd with heroic ardour at the sight,
And fearing every moment he would bite,
And rob our household of our only cat
That was of age to combat with a rat,
With outstretch'd hoe I slew him at the door,   40
And taught him NEVER TO COME THERE NO MORE.

Epitaph on a Hare

Here lies, whom hound did ne'er pursue,
    Nor swifter greyhound follow,
Whose foot ne'er tainted morning dew,
    Nor ear heard huntsman's hallo',

Old Tiney, surliest of his kind,
    Who, nurs'd with tender care,
And to domestic bounds confin'd,
    Was still a wild Jack-hare.

Though duly from my hand he took
    His pittance ev'ry night,   10
He did it with a jealous look,
    And, when he could, would bite.

His diet was of wheaten bread,
    And milk, and oats, and straw,
Thistles, or lettuces instead,
    With sand to scour his maw.

On twigs of hawthorn he regal'd,
    On pippins' russet peel;
And, when his juicy salads fail'd,
    Slic'd carrot pleas'd him well.   20

A Turkey carpet was his lawn,
    Whereon he lov'd to bound,
To skip and gambol like a fawn,
    And swing his rump around.

His frisking was at evening hours,
    For then he lost his fear;
But most before approaching show'rs,
    Or when a storm drew near.

Eight years and five round-rolling moons
    He thus saw steal away,   30
Dozing out all his idle noons,
    And ev'ry night at play.

I kept him for his humour's sake,
    For he would oft beguile
My heart of thoughts that made it ache,
    And force me to a smile.

But now, beneath this walnut shade
　　He finds his long, last home,
And waits, in snug concealment laid,
　　'Till gentler Puss shall come.　　　　　　40

He, still more aged, feels the shocks
　　From which no care can save,
And, partner once of Tiney's box,
　　Must soon partake his grave.

On the Death of
Mrs Throckmorton's Bulfinch

Ye nymphs, if e'er your eyes were red
With tears o'er hapless fav'rites shed,
　　O share Maria's grief!
Her fav'rite, even in his cage,
(What will not hunger's cruel rage?)
　　Assassin'd by a thief.

Where Rhenus strays his vines among,
The egg was laid from which he sprung,
　　And though by nature mute,
Or only with a whistle blest,　　　　　　10
Well-taught, he all the sounds express'd
　　Of flagelet or flute.

The honours of his ebon poll
Were brighter than the sleekest mole;
　　His bosom of the hue
With which Aurora decks the skies,
When piping winds shall soon arise
　　To sweep up all the dew.

Above, below, in all the house,
Dire foe, alike to bird and mouse, 20
    No cat had leave to dwell;
And Bully's cage supported stood,
On props of smoothest-shaven wood,
    Large-built and lattic'd well.

Well lattic'd – but the grate, alas!
Not rough with wire of steel or brass,
    For Bully's plumage sake,
But smooth with wands from Ouse's side,
With which, when neatly peel'd and dried,
    The swains their baskets make. 30

Night veil'd the pole – all seem'd secure –
When led by instinct sharp and sure,
    Subsistence to provide,
A beast forth sallied on the scout,
Long-back'd, long-tail'd, with whisker'd snout,
    And badger-colour'd hide.

He, ent'ring at the study door,
Its ample area 'gan explore;
    And something in the wind
Conjectur'd, sniffing round and round, 40
Better than all the books he found,
    Food, chiefly, for the mind.

Just then, by adverse fate impress'd,
A dream disturb'd poor Bully's rest;
    In sleep he seem'd to view
A rat, fast clinging to the cage,
And, screaming at the sad presage,
    Awoke and found it true.

For, aided both by ear and scent,
Right to his mark the monster went – 50
    Ah, Muse! forbear to speak
Minute the horrors that ensued;

His teeth were strong, the cage was wood –
    He left poor Bully's beak.

He left it – but he should have ta'en
That beak, whence issued many a strain
    Of such mellifluous tone,
Might have repaid him well, I wote,
For silencing so sweet a throat,
    Fast set within his own.   60

Maria weeps – the Muses mourn –
So, when by Bacchanalians torn,
    On Thracian Hebrus' side
The tree-enchanter Orpheus fell;
His head alone remain'd to tell
    The cruel death he died.

The Retired Cat

A poet's Cat, sedate and grave,
As poet well could wish to have,
Was much addicted to inquire
For nooks, to which she might retire,
And where, secure as mouse in chink,
She might repose, or sit and think.
I know not where she caught the trick –
Nature perhaps herself had cast her
In such a mould PHILOSOPHIQUE,
Or else she learn'd it of her Master.   10
Sometimes ascending, *debonair*,
An apple-tree, or lofty pear,
Lodg'd with convenience in the fork,
She watch'd the gardener at his work;
Sometimes her ease and solace sought
In an old empty watering-pot,
There wanting nothing, save a fan,
To seem some nymph in her sedan

Apparell'd in exactest sort,
And ready to be borne to court. 20
   But love of change it seems has place
Not only in our wiser race;
Cats also feel, as well as we,
That passion's force, and so did she.
Her climbing, she began to find,
Expos'd her too much to the wind,
And the old utensil of tin
Was cold and comfortless within:
She therefore wish'd instead of those,
Some place of more serene repose, 30
Where neither cold might come, nor air
Too rudely wanton with her hair,
And sought it in the likeliest mode
Within her master's snug abode.
   A draw'r, it chanc'd, at bottom lined
With linen of the softest kind,
With such as merchants introduce
From India, for the ladies' use,
A draw'r impending o'er the rest,
Half open in the topmost chest, 40
Of depth enough, and none to spare,
Invited her to slumber there.
Puss with delight beyond expression
Survey'd the scene, and took possession.
Recumbent at her ease ere long,
And lull'd by her own humdrum song,
She left the cares of life behind,
And slept as she would sleep her last,
When in came, housewifely inclined,
The chambermaid, and shut it fast, 50
By no malignity impell'd,
But all unconscious whom it held.
   Awaken'd by the shock, cried puss,
'Was ever cat attended thus!
The open drawer was left, I see,
Merely to prove a nest for me,
For soon as I was well compos'd

Then came the maid, and it was closed.
How smooth these 'kerchiefs and how sweet,
Oh what a delicate retreat!   60
I will resign myself to rest
Till Sol, declining in the west,
Shall call to supper, when, no doubt,
Susan will come and let me out'.
    The evening came, the sun descended,
And puss remain'd still unattended.
The night roll'd tardily away,
(With her indeed 'twas never day);
The sprightly morn her course renew'd,
The evening grey again ensued,   70
And puss came into mind no more
Than if entomb'd the day before.
With hunger pinch'd, and pinch'd for room,
She now presaged approaching doom,
Nor slept a single wink, or purr'd,
Conscious of jeopardy incurr'd.
    That night, by chance, the poet watching,
Heard an inexplicable scratching;
His noble heart went pit-a-pat,
And to himself he said – 'What's that?'   80
He drew the curtain at his side,
And forth he peep'd, but nothing spied;
Yet, by his ear directed, guess'd
Something imprison'd in the chest,
And, doubtful what, with prudent care,
Resolved it should continue there.
At length, a voice which well he knew,
A long and melancholy mew,
Saluting his poetic ears,
Consol'd him, and dispell'd his fears;   90
He left his bed, he trod the floor,
He 'gan in haste the draw'rs explore,
The lowest first, and without stop,
The rest in order to the top.
For 'tis a truth well known to most,
That whatsoever thing is lost,

We seek it, ere it come to light,
In ev'ry cranny but the right.
Forth skipp'd the cat; not now replete
As erst with airy self-conceit,   100
Nor in her own fond apprehension
A theme for all the world's attention,
But modest, sober, cured of all
Her notions hyperbolical,
And wishing for a place of rest
Any thing rather than a chest.
Then stepp'd the poet into bed
With this reflection in his head:

MORAL

Beware of too sublime a sense   110
Of your own worth and consequence.
The man who dreams himself so great,
And his importance of such weight,
That all around in all that's done
Must move and act for him alone,
Will learn in school of tribulation
The folly of his expectation.

To the Nightingale,

Which the Author heard sing on New Year's Day, 1792

Whence is it, that amaz'd I hear
   From yonder wither'd spray,
This foremost morn of all the year,
   The melody of May?

And why, since thousands would be proud
   Of such a favour shown,
Am I selected from the crowd,
   To witness it alone?

Sing'st thou, sweet Philomel, to me,
  For that I also long
Have practis'd in the groves like thee,
  Though not like thee in song?

Or sing'st thou rather under force
  Of some divine command,
Commission'd to presage a course
  Of happier days at hand?

Thrice welcome then! for many a long
  And joyless year have I,
As thou to-day, put forth my song
  Beneath a wintry sky.

But thee no wintry skies can harm,
  Who only need'st to sing,
To make even January charm,
  And ev'ry season Spring.

On a Spaniel, Called Beau,

Killing a young bird

A spaniel, Beau, that fares like you,
  Well fed, and at his ease,
Should wiser be than to pursue
  Each trifle that he sees.

But you have kill'd a tiny bird,
  Which flew not till to-day,
Against my orders, whom you heard
  Forbidding you the prey.

Nor did you kill, that you might eat,
  And ease a doggish pain,

For him, though chased with furious heat,
   You left where he was slain.

Nor was he of the thievish sort,
   Or one whom blood allures,
But innocent was all his sport,
   Whom you have torn for yours.

My dog! what remedy remains,
   Since, teach you all I can,
I see you, after all my pains,
   So much resemble man!

Beau's Reply

Sir, when I flew to seize the bird,
   In spite of your command,
A louder voice than yours I heard,
   And harder to withstand.

You cried – Forbear! – but in my breast
   A mightier cried – Proceed! –
'Twas nature, Sir, whose strong behest
   Impell'd me to the deed.

Yet much as nature I respect,
   I ventur'd once to break
(As you perhaps may recollect)
   Her precept, for your sake;

And when your linnet, on a day,
   Passing his prison door,
Had flutter'd all his strength away,
   And panting press'd the floor;

Well knowing him a sacred thing,
　　Not destin'd to my tooth,
I only kiss'd his ruffled wing,
　　And lick'd the feathers smooth.

Let my obedience then excuse
　　My disobedience now,
Nor some reproof yourself refuse
　　From your aggrieved bow-wow!

If killing birds be such a crime,
　　(Which I can hardly see)
What think you, Sir, of killing time
　　With verse address'd to me?

The Negro's Complaint

Forc'd from home and all its pleasures,
　　Afric's coast I left forlorn,
To increase the stranger's treasures,
　　O'er the raging billows borne.
Men from England bought and sold me,
　　Paid my price in paltry gold;
But, though slave they have enroll'd me,
　　Minds are never to be sold.

Still in thought as free as ever,
　　What are England's rights, I ask?   10
Me from my delights to sever,
　　Me to torture, me to task?
Fleecy locks, and black complexion
　　Cannot forfeit Nature's claim;
Skins may differ, but affection
　　Dwells in white and black the same.

Why did all-creating Nature
　　Make the plant for which we toil?

Sighs must fan it, tears must water,
   Sweat of ours must dress the soil.   20
Think, ye masters, iron-hearted,
   Lolling at your jovial boards;
Think how many backs have smarted
   For the sweets your cane affords.

Is there, as ye sometimes tell us,
   Is there one who reigns on high?
Has he bid you buy and sell us,
   Speaking from his throne, the sky?
Ask him, if your knotted scourges,
   Matches, blood-extorting screws,   30
Are the means that duty urges
   Agents of his will to use?

Hark! he answers – Wild tornadoes
   Strewing yonder sea with wrecks,
Wasting towns, plantations, meadows,
   Are the voice with which he speaks.
He, foreseeing what vexations
   Afric's sons should undergo,
Fix'd their tyrants' habitations
   Where his whirlwinds answer – No.   40

By our blood in Afric wasted,
   Ere our necks receiv'd the chain;
By the mis'ries that we tasted,
   Crossing in your barks the main;
By our suff'rings, since ye brought us
   To the man-degrading mart;
All sustain'd by patience, taught us
   Only by a broken heart!

Deem our nation brutes no longer,
   Till some reason ye shall find   50
Worthier of regard and stronger,
   Than the colour of our kind.
Slaves of gold, whose sordid dealings

Tarnish all your boasted pow'rs,
Prove that you have human feelings
Ere you proudly question ours!

Pity for Poor Africans

Video meliora proboque,
Deteriora sequor. –

I own I am shock'd at the purchase of slaves,
And fear those who buy them and sell them are knaves;
What I hear of their hardships, their tortures, and groans
Is almost enough to draw pity from stones.

I pity them greatly, but I must be mum,
For how could we do without sugar and rum?
Especially sugar, so needful we see;
What, give up our desserts, our coffee, and tea!

Besides, if we do, the French, Dutch, and Danes
Will heartily thank us, no doubt, for our pains;   10
If we do not buy the poor creatures, they will,
And tortures and groans will be multiplied still.

If foreigners likewise would give up the trade,
Much more in behalf of your wish might be said;
But, whilst they get riches by purchasing blacks,
Pray tell me why we may not also go snacks?

Your scruples and arguments bring to my mind
A story so pat, you may think it is coin'd,
On purpose to answer you, out of my mint;
But I can assure you, I saw it in print.   20

A youngster at school, more sedate than the rest,
Had once his integrity put to the test:

His comrades had plotted an orchard to rob,
And ask'd him to go and assist in the job.

He was shock'd, sir, like you, and answer'd – 'Oh, no!
What! rob our good neighbour? I pray you don't go!
Besides the man's poor, and his orchard's his bread:
Then think of his children, for they must be fed.'

'You talk very fine, and you look very grave,
But apples we want, and apples we'll have;   30
If you will go with us, we'll give you a share,
If not, you shall have neither apple nor pear.'

They ceas'd, and Tom ponder'd – 'I see they will go:
Poor man! what a pity to injure him so!
Poor man! I would save him his fruit if I could,
But staying behind them will do him no good.

'If the matter depended alone upon me,
His apples might hang till they dropp'd from the tree;
But since they will have them, I think I'll go too:
He will lose none by me, though I get a few.'   40

His scruples thus silenc'd, Tom felt more at ease,
And went with his comrades the apples to seize;
He blamed and protested, but join'd in the plan;
He shared in the plunder, but pitied the man.

The Morning Dream

'Twas in the glad season of spring,
    Asleep at the dawn of the day,
I dream'd what I cannot but sing,
    So pleasant it seem'd as I lay.
I dream'd that, on ocean afloat,
    Far hence to the westward I sail'd,

While the billows high-lifted the boat,
   And the fresh-blowing breeze never fail'd.

In the steerage a woman I saw,
   (Such at least was the form that she wore)
Whose beauty impress'd me with awe,
   Ne'er taught me by woman before.
She sat, and a shield at her side
   Shed light, like a sun on the waves,
And, smiling divinely, she cried –
   'I go to make freemen of slaves.'

Then raising her voice to a strain
   The sweetest that ear ever heard,
She sung of the slave's broken chain,
   Wherever her glory appear'd.
Some clouds, which had over us hung,
   Fled, chased by her melody clear,
And methought while she Liberty sung,
   'Twas Liberty only to hear.

Thus swiftly dividing the flood,
   To a slave-cultured island we came,
Where a Demon, her enemy, stood –
   Oppression his terrible name.
In his hand, as a sign of his sway,
   A scourge hung with lashes he bore,
And stood looking out for his prey
   From Africa's sorrowful shore.

But soon as approaching the land
   That goddess-like woman he view'd,
The scourge he let fall from his hand,
   With blood of his subjects imbrued.
I saw him both sicken and die,
   And the moment the monster expir'd,
Heard shouts that ascended the sky,
   From thousands with rapture inspired.

Awaking, how could I but muse
   At what such a dream should betide?

But soon my ear caught the glad news,
　　Which serv'd my weak thought for a guide –
That Britannia, renown'd o'er the waves
　　For the hatred she ever had shown
To the black-sceptred rulers of slaves,
　　Resolves to have none of her own.

Sweet Meat Has Sour Sauce:

Or, the Slave-trader in the Dumps

A trader I am to the African shore,
But since that my trading is like to be o'er,
I'll sing you a song that you ne'er heard before,
　　　　　Which nobody can deny, deny,
　　　　　Which nobody can deny.   5

When I first heard the news it gave me a shock,
Much like what they call an electrical knock,
And now I am going to sell off my stock,
　　　　　Which nobody can deny.

'Tis a curious assortment of dainty regales,   10
To tickle the negroes with when the ship sails,
Fine chains for the neck, and a cat with nine tails,
　　　　　Which nobody can deny.

Here's supple-jack plenty, and store of rat-tan,
That will wind itself round the sides of a man,   15
As close as a hoop around a bucket or can,
　　　　　Which nobody can deny.

Here's padlocks and bolts, and screws for the thumbs,
That squeeze them so lovingly till the blood comes;
They sweeten the temper like comfits or plums,   20
　　　　　Which nobody can deny.

When a negro his head from his victuals withdraws,
And clenches his teeth and thrusts out his paws,
Here's a notable engine to open his jaws,
    Which nobody can deny.   25

Thus going to market, we kindly prepare
A pretty black cargo of African ware,
For what they must meet with when they get there,
    Which nobody can deny.

'Twould do your heart good to see 'em below   30
Lie flat on their backs all the way as we go,
Like sprats on a gridiron, scores in a row,
    Which nobody can deny.

But ah! if in vain I have studied an art
So gainful to me, all boasting apart,
I think it will break my compassionate heart, 35
    Which nobody can deny.

For oh! how it enters my soul like an awl!
This pity, which some people self-pity call,
Is sure the most heart-piercing pity of all, 40
    Which nobody can deny.

So this is my song, as I told you before;
Come, buy off my stock, for I must no more
Carry Cæsars and Pompeys to Sugar-cane shore,
    Which nobody can deny, deny, 45
    Which nobody can deny.

from **Olney Hymns**

The Contrite Heart
Isa. lvii. 15

The Lord will happiness divine
   On contrite hearts bestow:
Then tell me, gracious God, is mine
   A contrite heart, or no?

I hear, but seem to hear in vain,
   Insensible as steel;
If ought is felt, 'tis only pain,
   To find I cannot feel.

I sometimes think myself inclin'd
   To love thee, if I could;
But often feel another mind,
   Averse to all that's good.

My best desires are faint and few,
   I fain would strive for more;
But when I cry, 'My strength renew!'
   Seem weaker than before.

Thy saints are comforted I know,
   And love thy house of pray'r;
I therefore go where others go,
   But find no comfort there.

O make this heart rejoice, or ache;
   Decide this doubt for me;
And if it be not broken, break, –
   And heal it if it be.

Contentment
Phil. iv. 11

Fierce passions discompose the mind,
    As tempests vex the sea;
But calm content and peace we find,
    When, Lord, we turn to thee.

In vain by reason and by rule
    We try to bend the will;
For none but in the Saviour's school
    Can learn the heav'nly skill.

Since at his feet my soul has sat,
    His gracious words to hear;
Contented with my present state,
    I cast, on him, my care.

'Art thou a sinner, soul?' he said,
    'Then how canst thou complain?
How light thy troubles here, if weigh'd
    With everlasting pain!

'If thou of murmuring wouldst be cur'd,
    Compare thy griefs with mine;
Think what my love for thee endur'd,
    And thou wilt not repine.

''Tis I appoint thy daily lot,
    And I do all things well:
Thou soon shalt leave this wretched spot,
    And rise with me to dwell.

'In life my grace shall strength supply,
    Proportion'd to thy day;
At death thou shalt find me nigh,
    To wipe thy tears away.'

Thus I, who once my wretched days
    In vain repinings spent,
Taught in my Saviour's school of grace,
    Have learn'd to be content.

xxxv   ## Light Shining out of Darkness

God moves in a mysterious way,
    His wonders to perform;
He plants his footsteps in the sea,
    And rides upon the storm.

Deep in unfathomable mines
    Of never failing skill,
He treasures up his bright designs,
    And works his sovereign will.

Ye fearful saints fresh courage take,
    The clouds ye so much dread
Are big with mercy, and shall break
    In blessings on your head.

Judge not the Lord by feeble sense,
    But trust him for his grace,
Behind a frowning providence
    He hides a smiling face.

His purposes will ripen fast,
    Unfolding ev'ry hour;
The bud may have a bitter taste,
    But sweet will be the flow'r.

Blind unbelief is sure to err,
   And scan his work in vain;
God is his own interpreter,
   And he will make it plain.

Temptation

The billows swell, the winds are high,
Clouds overcast my wintry sky;
Out of the depths to thee I call,
My fears are great, my strength is small.

O Lord, the pilot's part perform,
And guard and guide me through the storm;
Defend me from each threatening ill,
Control the waves, – say, 'Peace! be still.'

Amidst the roaring of the sea,
My soul still hangs her hope on thee;
Thy constant love, thy faithful care,
Is all that saves me from despair.

Dangers of ev'ry shape and name
Attend the followers of the Lamb,
Who leave the world's deceitful shore,
And leave it to return no more.

Tho' tempest-toss'd and half a wreck,
My Saviour thro' the floods I seek;
Let neither winds nor stormy main,
Force back my shatter'd bark again.

On the Receipt of my Mother's Picture

Out of Norfolk,
The Gift of My Cousin, Anne Bodham

O that those lips had language! Life has pass'd
With me but roughly since I heard thee last.
Those lips are thine – thy own sweet smiles I see,
The same that oft in childhood solaced me;
Voice only fails, else how distinct they say,
'Grieve not, my child, chase all thy fears away!'
The meek intelligence of those dear eyes
(Blest be the art that can immortalize,
The art that baffles time's tyrannic claim
To quench it) here shines on me still the same.   10
      Faithful remembrancer of one so dear,
Oh welcome guest, though unexpected here!
Who bidst me honour with an artless song,
Affectionate, a mother lost so long,
I will obey, not willingly alone,
But gladly, as the precept were her own;
And, while that face renews my filial grief,
Fancy shall weave a charm for my relief –
Shall steep me in Elysian reverie,
A momentary dream, that thou art she.   20
      My mother! when I learn'd that thou wast dead,
Say, wast thou conscious of the tears I shed?
Hover'd thy spirit o'er thy sorrowing son,
Wretch even then, life's journey just begun?
Perhaps thou gavest me, though unfelt, a kiss;
Perhaps a tear, if souls can weep in bliss –
Ah, that maternal smile! – it answers – Yes.
I heard the bell toll'd on thy burial day,
I saw the hearse that bore thee slow away,
And, turning from my nurs'ry window, drew   30
A long, long sigh, and wept a last adieu!
But was it such? – It was. – Where thou art gone
Adieus and farewells are a sound unknown.
May I but meet thee on that peaceful shore,
The parting word shall pass my lips no more!

Thy maidens, griev'd themselves at my concern,
Oft gave me promise of thy quick return.
What ardently I wish'd, I long believ'd,
And, disappointed still, was still deceiv'd;
By expectation every day beguiled,   40
Dupe of to-morrow even from a child.
Thus many a sad to-morrow came and went,
Till, all my stock of infant sorrow spent,
I learn'd at last submission to my lot;
But, though I less deplor'd thee, ne'er forgot.

Where once we dwelt our name is heard no more,
Children not thine have trod my nurs'ry floor;
And where the gard'ner Robin, day by day,
Drew me to school along the public way,
Delighted with my bauble coach, and wrapt   50
In scarlet mantle warm, and velvet capt,
'Tis now become a history little known,
That once we call'd the past'ral house our own.
Shortliv'd possession! but the record fair,
That mem'ry keeps of all thy kindness there,
Still outlives many a storm that has effac'd
A thousand other themes less deeply trac'd.
Thy nightly visits to my chamber made,
That thou mightst know me safe and warmly laid;
Thy morning bounties ere I left my home,   60
The biscuit, or confectionary plum;
The fragrant waters on my cheeks bestow'd
By thy own hand, till fresh they shone and glow'd:
All this, and more endearing still than all,
Thy constant flow of love, that knew no fall,
Ne'er roughen'd by those cataracts and breaks,
That humour interpos'd too often makes;
All this still legible in mem'ry's page,
And still to be so, to my latest age,
Adds joy to duty, makes me glad to pay   70
Such honours to thee as my numbers may;
Perhaps a frail memorial, but sincere,
Not scorn'd in heaven, though little notic'd here.

Could Time, his flight revers'd, restore the hours,
When, playing with thy vesture's tissued flow'rs,

The violet, the pink, and jessamine,
I prick'd them into paper with a pin,
(And thou wast happier than myself the while,
Wouldst softly speak, and stroke my head, and smile,)
Could those few pleasant days again appear,   80
Might one wish bring them, would I wish them here?
I would not trust my heart – the dear delight
Seems so to be desir'd, perhaps I might –
But no – what here we call our life is such,
So little to be loved, and thou so much,
That I should ill requite thee to constrain
Thy unbound spirit into bonds again.
      Thou, as a gallant bark from Albion's coast
(The storms all weather'd, and the ocean cross'd)
Shoots into port at some well-haven'd isle,   90
Where spices breathe, and brighter seasons smile,
There sits quiescent on the floods, that show
Her beauteous form reflected clear below,
While airs impregnated with incense play
Around her, fanning light her streamers gay;
So thou, with sails how swift! hast reach'd the shore,
'Where tempests never beat nor billows roar,'
And thy lov'd consort on the dang'rous tide
Of life, long since, has anchor'd by thy side.
But me, scarce hoping to attain that rest,   100
Always from port withheld, always distress'd –
Me howling winds drive devious, tempest-toss'd,
Sails ripp'd, seams op'ning wide, and compass lost,
And day by day some current's thwarting force
Sets me more distant from a prosperous course.
Yet O the thought, that thou art safe, and he!
That thought is joy, arrive what may to me.
My boast is not that I deduce my birth
From loins enthron'd and rulers of the earth;
But higher far my proud pretensions rise –   110
The son of parents pass'd into the skies.
And now, farewell – Time unrevoked has run
His wonted course, yet what I wish'd is done.
By contemplation's help, not sought in vain,
I seem t' have liv'd my childhood o'er again;

To have renew'd the joys that once were mine,
Without the sin of violating thine;
And, while the wings of fancy still are free,
And I can view this mimic show of thee,
Time has but half succeeded in his theft –   120
Thyself remov'd, thy power to soothe me left.

To Mary

The twentieth year is well-nigh past,
Since first our sky was overcast –
Ah would that this might be the last!
                    My Mary!

Thy spirits have a fainter flow,
I see thee daily weaker grow –
'Twas my distress that brought thee low,
                    My Mary!

Thy needles, once a shining store,
For my sake restless heretofore,   10
Now rust disus'd, and shine no more,
                    My Mary!

For though thou gladly wouldst fulfil
The same kind office for me still,
Thy sight now seconds not thy will,
                    My Mary!

But well thou play'dst the housewife's part,
And all thy threads with magic art
Have wound themselves about this heart,
                    My Mary!   20

Thy indistinct expressions seem
Like language utter'd in a dream;
Yet me they charm, whate'er the theme,
                    My Mary!

Thy silver locks, once auburn bright,
Are still more lovely in my sight
Than golden beams of orient light,
                    My Mary!

For could I view nor them nor thee,
What sight worth seeing could I see?   30
The sun would rise in vain for me,
                    My Mary!

Partakers of thy sad decline,
Thy hands their little force resign;
Yet, gently prest, press gently mine,
                    My Mary!

And then I feel that still I hold
A richer store ten thousandfold
Than misers fancy in their gold,
                    My Mary!   40

Such feebleness of limbs thou prov'st,
That now at every step thou mov'st
Upheld by two, yet still thou lov'st,
                    My Mary!

And still to love, though prest with ill,
In wintry age to feel no chill,
With me is to be lovely still,
                    My Mary!

But ah! by constant heed I know,
How oft the sadness that I show,   50
Transforms thy smiles to looks of woe,
                    My Mary!

And should my future lot be cast
With much resemblance of the past,
Thy worn-out heart will break at last,
                    My Mary!

from **The Task**

from **Book I: The Sofa**

Scenes that sooth'd

Or charm'd me young, no longer young, I find
Still soothing and of pow'r to charm me still.
And witness, dear companion of my walks,
Whose arm this twentieth winter I perceive 145
Fast lock'd in mine, with pleasure such as love
Confirm'd by long experience of thy worth
And well-tried virtues could alone inspire –
Witness a joy that thou hast doubled long.
Thou know'st my praise of nature most sincere,   150
And that my raptures are not conjur'd up
To serve occasions of poetic pomp,
But genuine, and art partner of them all.
How oft upon yon eminence our pace
Has slacken'd to a pause, and we have borne   155
The ruffling wind, scarce conscious that it blew,
While admiration feeding at the eye,
And still unsated, dwelt upon the scene.
Thence with what pleasure have we just discern'd
The distant plough slow moving, and beside   160
His lab'ring team, that swerved not from the track,
The sturdy swain diminish'd to a boy!
Here Ouse, slow winding through a level plain
Of spacious meads with cattle sprinkled o'er,
Conducts the eye along his sinuous course   165
Delighted. There, fast rooted in his bank,
Stand, never overlook'd, our fav'rite elms
That screen the herdsman's solitary hut;
While far beyond, and overthwart the stream
That, as with molten glass, inlays the vale,   170
The sloping land recedes into the clouds;
Displaying on its varied side the grace
Of hedge-row beauties numberless, square tow'r,

Tall spire, from which the sound of cheerful bells
Just undulates upon the list'ning ear,   175
Groves, heaths, and smoking villages remote.
Scenes must be beautiful, which daily view'd,
Please daily, and whose novelty survives
Long knowledge and the scrutiny of years.
Praise justly due to those that I describe.   180
    Nor rural sights alone, but rural sounds
Exhilarate the spirit, and restore
The tone of languid Nature. Mighty winds,
That sweep the skirt of some far-spreading wood
Of ancient growth, make music not unlike   185
The dash of ocean on his winding shore,
And lull the spirit while they fill the mind,
Unnumber'd branches waving in the blast,
And all their leaves fast flutt'ring, all at once.
Nor less composure waits upon the roar   190
Of distant floods, or on the softer voice
Of neighb'ring fountain, or of rills that slip
Through the cleft rock, and chiming as they fall
Upon loose pebbles, lose themselves at length
In matted grass, that with a livelier green   195
Betrays the secret of their silent course.
Nature inanimate employs sweet sounds,
But animated Nature sweeter still
To soothe and satisfy the human ear.
Ten thousand warblers cheer the day, and one   200
The live-long night: nor these alone, whose notes
Nice-finger'd art must emulate in vain,
But cawing rooks, and kites that swim sublime
In still repeated circles, screaming loud,
The jay, the pie, and ev'n the boding owl   205
That hails the rising moon, have charms for me.
Sounds inharmonious in themselves and harsh,
Yet heard in scenes where peace for ever reigns,
And only there, please highly for their sake.
    Peace to the artist, whose ingenious thought   210
Devis'd the weather-house, that useful toy!
Fearless of humid air and gathering rains,

Forth steps the man – an emblem of myself;
More delicate his timorous mate retires.
When Winter soaks the fields, and female feet,   215
Too weak to struggle with tenacious clay,
Or ford the rivulets, are best at home,
The task of new discov'ries falls on me.
At such a season and with such a charge
Once went I forth, and found, till then unknown,   220
A cottage, whither oft we since repair:
'Tis perch'd upon the green-hill top, but close
Environ'd with a ring of branching elms
That overhang the thatch, itself unseen,
Peeps at the vale below; so thick beset   225
With foliage of such dark redundant growth,
I call'd the low-roof'd lodge the *peasant's nest.*
And, hidden as it is, and far remote
From such unpleasing sounds as haunt the ear
In village or in town, the bay of curs   230
Incessant, clinking hammers, grinding wheels,
And infants clam'rous whether pleas'd or pain'd,
Oft have I wish'd the peaceful covert mine.
Here, I have said, at least I should possess
The poet's treasure, silence, and indulge   235
The dreams of fancy, tranquil and secure.
Vain thought! the dweller in that still retreat
Dearly obtains the refuge it affords.
Its elevated site forbids the wretch
To drink sweet waters of the crystal well;   240
He dips his bowl into the weedy ditch,
And, heavy-laden, brings his bev'rage home,
Far-fetch'd and little worth; nor seldom waits,
Dependent on the baker's punctual call,
To hear his creaking panniers at the door,   245
Angry and sad, and his last crust consumed.
So farewell envy of the *peasant's nest.*
If solitude make scant the means of life,
Society for me! Thou seeming sweet,
Be still a pleasing object in my view;   250
My visit still, but never mine abode.

Descending now (but cautious, lest too fast)
A sudden steep, upon a rustic bridge
We pass a gulf in which the willows dip
Their pendent boughs, stooping as if to drink.
Hence ancle-deep in moss and flow'ry thyme,   270
We mount again, and feel at ev'ry step
Our foot half sunk in hillocks green and soft,
Raised by the mole, the miner of the soil.
He, not unlike the great ones of mankind,
Disfigures earth, and, plotting in the dark,   275
Toils much to earn a monumental pile,
That may record the mischiefs he has done.
    The summit gain'd, behold the proud alcove
That crowns it! yet not all its pride secures
The grand retreat from injuries impress'd   280
By rural carvers, who with knives deface
The panels, leaving an obscure, rude name
In characters uncouth, and spelt amiss.
So strong the zeal t' immortalize himself
Beats in the breast of man, that ev'n a few   285
Few transient years won from th' abyss abhorr'd
Of blank oblivion, seem a glorious prize,
And even to a clown. Now roves the eye;
And posted on this speculative height
Exults in its command. The sheep-fold here   290
Pours out its fleecy tenants o'er the glebe,
At first, progressive as a stream, they seek
The middle field; but scatter'd by degrees
Each to his choice, soon whiten all the land.
There, from the sun-burnt hay-field homeward creeps   295
The loaded wain, while lighten'd of its charge
The wain that meets it passes swiftly by,
The boorish driver leaning o'er his team
Vocif'rous, and impatient of delay.
Nor less attractive is the woodland scene,   300
Diversified with trees of every growth,
Alike yet various. Here the grey smooth trunks
Of ash, or lime, or beech, distinctly shine,
Within the twilight of their distant shades;

There, lost behind a rising ground, the wood 305
Seems sunk, and shorten'd to its topmost boughs.
No tree in all the grove but has its charms,
Though each its hue peculiar; paler some,
And of a wannish grey; the willow such
And poplar, that with silver lines his leaf, 310
And ash far-stretching his umbrageous arm;
Of deeper green the elm; and deeper still,
Lord of the woods, the long-surviving oak.
Some glossy-leav'd and shining in the sun,
The maple, and the beech of oily nuts 315
Prolific, and the lime at dewy eve
Diffusing odours: nor unnoted pass
The sycamore, capricious in attire,
Now green, now tawny, and ere autumn yet
Have changed the woods, in scarlet honours bright. 320
O'er these, but far beyond, (a spacious map
Of hill and valley interpos'd between,)
The Ouse, dividing the well-water'd land,
Now glitters in the sun, and now retires,
As bashful, yet impatient to be seen. 325

Like a coy maiden, ease, when courted most,
Farthest retires – an idol, at whose shrine 410
Who oft'nest sacrifice are favour'd least.
The love of Nature, and the scenes she draws,
Is Nature's dictate. Strange! there should be found
Who self-imprison'd in their proud saloons,
Renounce the odours of the open field 415
For the unscented fictions of the loom;
Who satisfied with only pencil'd scenes,
Prefer to the performance of a God
Th' inferior wonders of an artist's hand.
Lovely indeed the mimic works of art, 420
But Nature's works far lovelier. I admire –
None more admires – the painter's magic skill
Who shows me that which I shall never see,
Conveys a distant country into mine,
And throws Italian light on English walls. 425

But imitative strokes can do no more
Than please the eye, sweet Nature every sense.
The air salubrious of her lofty hills,
The cheering fragrance of her dewy vales,
And music of her woods – no works of man   430
May rival these; these all bespeak a pow'r
Peculiar, and exclusively her own.
Beneath the open sky she spreads the feast;
'Tis free to all – 'tis every day renew'd;
Who scorns it, starves deservedly at home.   435
He does not scorn it, who imprison'd long
In some unwholesome dungeon, and a prey
To sallow sickness, which the vapours dank
And clammy of his dark abode have bred,
Escapes at last to liberty and light.   440
His cheek recovers soon its healthful hue,
His eye relumines its extinguish'd fires,
He walks, he leaps, he runs – is wing'd with joy,
And riots in the sweets of ev'ry breeze.

   There often wanders one, whom better days
Saw better clad, in cloak of satin trimm'd   535
With lace, and hat with splendid riband bound.
A serving-maid was she, and fell in love
With one who left her, went to sea, and died.
Her fancy follow'd him through foaming waves
To distant shores; and she would sit and weep   540
At what a sailor suffers; fancy too,
Delusive most where warmest wishes are,
Would oft anticipate his glad return,
And dream of transports she was not to know.
She heard the doleful tidings of his death –   545
And never smil'd again. And now she roams
The dreary waste; there spends the livelong day,
And there, unless when charity forbids,
The livelong night. A tatter'd apron hides,
Worn as a cloak, and hardly hides a gown   550
More tatter'd still; and both but ill conceal
A bosom heav'd with never-ceasing sighs.

She begs an idle pin of all she meets,
And hoards them in her sleeve; but needful food,
Though press'd with hunger oft, or comelier clothes,   555
Though pinch'd with cold, asks never. – Kate is craz'd.
   I see a column of slow rising smoke
O'ertop the lofty wood that skirts the wild.
A vagabond and useless tribe there eat
Their miserable meal. A kettle slung   560
Between two poles upon a stick transverse,
Receives the morsel; flesh obscene of dog,
Or vermin, or at best, of cock purloin'd
From his accustom'd perch. Hard faring race!
They pick their fuel out of ev'ry hedge,   565
Which, kindled with dry leaves, just saves unquench'd
The spark of life. The sportive wind blows wide
Their flutt'ring rags, and shows a tawny skin,
The vellum of the pedigree they claim.
Great skill have they in palmistry, and more   570
To conjure clean away the gold they touch,
Conveying worthless dross into its place.
Loud when they beg, dumb only when they steal.
Strange! that a creature rational, and cast
In human mould, should brutalize by choice   575
His nature, and though capable of arts
By which the world might profit and himself,
Self-banish'd from society, prefer
Such squalid sloth to honourable toil.
Yet even these, though feigning sickness oft   580
They swathe the forehead, drag the limping limb,
And vex their flesh with artificial sores,
Can change their whine into a mirthful note
When safe occasion offers, and with dance,
And music of the bladder and the bag,   585
Beguile their woes and make the woods resound.
Such health and gaiety of heart enjoy
The houseless rovers of the sylvan world;
And, breathing wholesome air, and wand'ring much,
Need other physic none to heal th' effects   590
Of loathsome diet, penury, and cold.

Even the favour'd isles, 620
So lately found, although the constant sun
Cheer all their seasons with a grateful smile,
Can boast but little virtue; and, inert
Through plenty, lose in morals what they gain
In manners, victims of luxurious ease. 625
These therefore I can pity, plac'd remote
From all that science traces, art invents,
Or inspiration teaches; and enclosed
In boundless oceans never to be pass'd
By navigators uninform'd as they, 630
Or plough'd perhaps by British bark again.
But far beyond the rest, and with most cause,
Thee, gentle savage! whom no love of thee
Or thine, but curiosity perhaps,
Or else vain glory, prompted us to draw 635
Forth from thy native bow'rs, to show thee here
With what superior skill we can abuse
The gifts of Providence, and squander life.
The dream is past. And thou hast found again
Thy cocoas and bananas, palms and yams, 640
And homestall thatch'd with leaves. But hast thou found
Their former charms? And, having seen our state,
Our palaces, our ladies, and our pomp
Of equipage, our gardens, and our sports,
And heard our music; are thy simple friends, 645
Thy simple fare, and all thy plain delights
As dear to thee as once? And have thy joys
Lost nothing by comparison with ours?
Rude as thou art (for we return'd thee rude
And ignorant except of outward show) 650
I cannot think thee yet so dull of heart
And spiritless, as never to regret
Sweets tasted here, and left as soon as known.
Methinks I see thee straying on the beach,
And asking of the surge that bathes thy foot 655
If ever it has washed our distant shore.
I see thee weep, and thine are honest tears,
A patriot's for his country. Thou art sad

At thought of her forlorn and abject state,
From which no pow'r of thine can raise her up. 660
Thus fancy paints thee, and though apt to err,
Perhaps errs little, when she paints thee thus.
She tells me too, that duly ev'ry morn
Thou climb'st the mountain top, with eager eye
Exploring far and wide the wat'ry waste 665
For sight of ship from England. Ev'ry speck
Seen in the dim horizon, turns thee pale
With conflict of contending hopes and fears.
But comes at last the dull and dusky eve,
And sends thee to thy cabin well-prepar'd 670
To dream all night of what the day denied.
Alas! expect it not. We found no bait
To tempt us in thy country. Doing good,
Disinterested good, is not our trade.
We travel far 'tis true, but not for nought; 675
And must be brib'd to compass earth again,
By other hopes and richer fruits than yours.

God made the country, and man made the town.
What wonder then, that health and virtue, gifts 750
That can alone make sweet the bitter draught
That life holds out to all, should most abound
And least be threaten'd in the fields and groves?
Possess ye therefore, ye who, borne about
In chariots and sedans, know no fatigue 755
But that of idleness, and taste no scenes
But such as art contrives – possess ye still
Your element; there only ye can shine,
There only minds like yours can do no harm.
Our groves were planted to console at noon 760
The pensive wand'rer in their shades. At eve
The moon-beam sliding softly in between
The sleeping leaves, is all the light they wish,
Birds warbling all the music. We can spare
The splendour of your lamps, they but eclipse 765
Our softer satellite. Your songs confound
Our more harmonious notes. The thrush departs

Scar'd, and th' offended nightingale is mute.
There is a public mischief in your mirth;
It plagues your country. Folly such as yours,   770
Grac'd with a sword, and worthier of a fan,
Has made, what enemies could ne'er have done,
Our arch of empire, steadfast but for you,
A mutilated structure, soon to fall.

from **Book II: The Time-Piece**

Oh for a lodge in some vast wilderness,
Some boundless contiguity of shade,
Where rumour of oppression and deceit,
Of unsuccessful or successful war
Might never reach me more. My ear is pain'd,   5
My soul is sick with ev'ry day's report
Of wrong and outrage with which earth is fill'd.
There is no flesh in man's obdurate heart,
It does not feel for man. The natural bond
Of brotherhood is sever'd as the flax   10
That falls asunder at the touch of fire.
He finds his fellow guilty of a skin
Not colour'd like his own, and having power
T' enforce the wrong, for such a worthy cause
Dooms and devotes him as his lawful prey.   15
Lands intersected by a narrow frith
Abhor each other. Mountains interpos'd,
Make enemies of nations who had else,
Like kindred drops, been mingled into one.
Thus man devotes his brother, and destroys;   20
And worse than all, and most to be deplored
As human nature's broadest, foulest blot,
Chains him, and tasks him, and exacts his sweat
With stripes, that mercy with a bleeding heart,
Weeps when she sees inflicted on a beast.   25
Then what is man? And what man, seeing this,

And having human feelings, does not blush
And hang his head, to think himself a man?
I would not have a slave to till my ground,
To carry me, to fan me while I sleep,   30
And tremble when I wake, for all the wealth
That sinews bought and sold have ever earn'd.
No: dear as freedom is, and in my heart's
Just estimation prized above all price,
I had much rather be myself the slave,   35
And wear the bonds, than fasten them on him.
We have no slaves at home – Then why abroad?
And they themselves once ferried o'er the wave
That parts us, are mancipate and loosed.
Slaves cannot breathe in England; if their lungs   40
Receive our air, that moment they are free;
They touch our country and their shackles fall.
That's noble, and bespeaks a nation proud
And jealous of the blessing. Spread it then,
And let it circulate through every vein   45
Of all your empire! that where Britain's pow'r
Is felt, mankind may feel her mercy too.

A man o' th' town dines late, but soon enough,
With reasonable forecast and dispatch,
T' insure a side-box station at half price.
You think, perhaps, so delicate his dress,   625
His daily fare as delicate. Alas!
He picks clean teeth, and, busy as he seems
With an old tavern quill, is hungry yet.
The rout is folly's circle, which she draws
With magic wand. So potent is the spell,   630
That none, decoy'd into that fatal ring,
Unless by heav'n's peculiar grace, escape.
There we grow early grey, but never wise;
There form connexions, but acquire no friend;
Solicit pleasure, hopeless of success;   635
Waste youth in occupations only fit
For second childhood, and devote old age
To sports which only childhood could excuse.
There they are happiest who dissemble best

Their weariness; and they the most polite   640
Who squander time and treasure with a smile,
Though at their own destruction. She that asks
Her dear five hundred friends, contemns them all,
And hates their coming. They (what can they less?)
Make just reprisals, and with cringe and shrug   645
And bow obsequious, hide their hate of her.
All catch the frenzy, downward from her Grace,
Whose flambeaux flash against the morning skies,
And gild our chamber ceilings as they pass,
To her who, frugal only that her thrift   650
May feed excesses she can ill afford,
Is hackney'd home unlackey'd – who in haste
Alighting, turns the key in her own door,
And at the watchman's lantern borrowing light,
Finds a cold bed her only comfort left.   655
Wives beggar husbands, husbands starve their wives,
On fortune's velvet altar offering up
Their last poor pittance – fortune most severe
Of goddesses yet known, and costlier far
Than all that held their routs in Juno's heav'n –   660
So fare we in this prison-house the world:
And 'tis a fearful spectacle to see
So many maniacs dancing in their chains.
They gaze upon the links that hold them fast
With eyes of anguish, execrate their lot,   665
Then shake them in despair, and dance again.

from **Book III: The Garden**

   I was a stricken deer, that left the herd
Long since; with many an arrow deep infixt
My panting side was charg'd when I withdrew   110
To seek a tranquil death in distant shades.
There was I found by one who had himself
Been hurt by th' archers. In his side he bore

And in his hands and feet, the cruel scars.
With gentle force soliciting the darts   115
He drew them forth, and heal'd and bade me live.
Since then, with few associates, in remote
And silent woods I wander, far from those
My former partners of the peopled scene,
With few associates, and not wishing more.   120
Here much I ruminate, as much I may,
With other views of men and manners now
Than once, and others of a life to come.
I see that all are wand'rers, gone astray,
Each in his own delusions; they are lost   125
In chase of fancied happiness, still woo'd
And never won. Dream after dream ensues;
And still they dream that they shall still succeed,
And still are disappointed. Rings the world
With the vain stir. I sum up half mankind,   130
And add two thirds of the remainder half,
And find the total of their hopes and fears
Dreams, empty dreams. The million flit as gay
As if created only like the fly
That spreads his motley wings in th' eye of noon,   135
To sport their season, and be seen no more.
The rest are sober dreamers, grave and wise,
And pregnant with discov'ries new and rare.
Some write a narrative of wars and feats
Of heroes little known, and call the rant   140
An history; describe the man, of whom
His own coevals took but little note,
And paint his person, character and views,
As they had known him from his mother's womb.
They disentangle from the puzzled skein   145
In which obscurity has wrapp'd them up,
The threads of politic and shrewd design
That ran through all his purposes, and charge
His mind with meanings that he never had,
Or having, kept conceal'd. Some drill and bore   150
The solid earth, and from the strata there
Extract a register, by which we learn
That he who made it and reveal'd its date

To Moses, was mistaken in its age.
Some, more acute, and more industrious still,   155
Contrive creation; travel nature up
To the sharp peak of her sublimest height,
And tell us whence the stars; why some are fix'd,
And planetary some; what gave them first
Rotation, from what fountain flow'd their light.   160
Great contest follows, and much learned dust
Involves the combatants; each claiming truth,
And truth disclaiming both. And thus they spend
The little wick of life's poor shallow lamp,
In playing tricks with nature, giving laws   165
To distant worlds, and trifling in their own.
Is't not a pity now that tickling rheums
Should ever tease the lungs and blear the sight
Of oracles like these? Great pity too,
That having wielded th' elements, and built   170
A thousand systems, each in his own way,
They should go out in fume and be forgot?
Ah! what is life thus spent? and what are they
But frantic who thus spend it? all for smoke –
Eternity for bubbles, proves at last   175
A senseless bargain. When I see such games
Play'd by the creatures of a pow'r who swears
That he will judge the earth, and call the fool
To a sharp reck'ning that has liv'd in vain;
And when I weigh this seeming wisdom well,   180
And prove it in the infallible result
So hollow and so false – I feel my heart
Dissolve in pity, and account the learn'd,
If this be learning, most of all deceiv'd.
Great crimes alarm the conscience, but she sleeps   185
While thoughtful man is plausibly amus'd.
Defend me, therefore, common sense, say I,
From dropping buckets into empty wells,
And growing old in drawing nothing up!   190

    Oh friendly to the best pursuits of man,   290
Friendly to thought, to virtue, and to peace,
Domestic life in rural leisure pass'd!

Few know thy value, and few taste thy sweets,
Though many boast thy favours, and affect
To understand and chuse thee for their own.   295
But foolish man foregoes his proper bliss
Ev'n as his first progenitor, and quits,
Though placed in paradise, (for earth has still
Some traces of her youthful beauty left)
Substantial happiness for transient joy.   300
Scenes form'd for contemplation, and to nurse
The growing seeds of wisdom; that suggest
By ev'ry pleasing image they present
Reflections such as meliorate the heart,
Compose the passions and exalt the mind;   305
Scenes such as these, 'tis his supreme delight
To fill with riot, and defile with blood.
Should some contagion, kind to the poor brutes
We persecute, annihilate the tribes
That draw the sportsman over hill and dale   310
Fearless, and rapt away from all his cares;
Should never game-fowl hatch her eggs again,
Nor baited hook deceive the fish's eye;
Could pageantry and dance and feast and song
Be quell'd in all our summer-month retreats;   315
How many self-deluded nymphs and swains,
Who dream they have a taste for fields and groves,
Would find them hideous nurs'ries of the spleen,
And crowd the roads, impatient for the town!
They love the country, and none else, who seek   320
For their own sake its silence and its shade;
Delights which who would leave, that has a heart
Susceptible of pity, or a mind
Cultur'd and capable of sober thought,
For all the savage din of the swift pack,   325
And clamours of the field? Detested sport,
That owes its pleasures to another's pain;
That feeds upon the sobs and dying shrieks
Of harmless nature, dumb, but yet endu'd
With eloquence that agonies inspire,   330
Of silent tears and heart-distending sighs!
Vain tears alas! and sighs that never find

A corresponding tone in jovial souls.
Well – one at least is safe. One shelter'd hare
Has never heard the sanguinary yell   335
Of cruel man, exulting in her woes.
Innocent partner of my peaceful home,
Whom ten long years' experience of my care
Has made at last familiar, she has lost
Much of her vigilant instinctive dread,   340
Not needful here, beneath a roof like mine.
Yes – thou may'st eat thy bread, and lick the hand
That feeds thee; thou may'st frolic on the floor
At evening, and at night retire secure
To thy straw couch, and slumber unalarm'd.   345
For I have gain'd thy confidence, have pledg'd
All that is human in me, to protect
Thine unsuspecting gratitude and love.
If I survive thee I will dig thy grave;
And when I place thee in it, sighing say,   350
I knew at least one hare that had a friend.

The morning finds the self-sequester'd man
Fresh for his task, intend what task he may.
Whether inclement seasons recommend
His warm but simple home, where he enjoys
With her who shares his pleasures and his heart,   390
Sweet converse, sipping calm the fragrant lymph
Which neatly she prepares; then to his book
Well chosen, and not sullenly perús'd
In selfish silence, but imparted oft
As aught occurs that she may smile to hear,   395
Or turn to nourishment, digested well.
Or if the garden with its many cares,
All well repaid, demand him, he attends
The welcome call, conscious how much the hand
Of lubbard labour needs his watchful eye,   400
Oft loit'ring lazily if not o'erseen,
Or misapplying his unskilful strength.
Nor does he govern only or direct,
But much performs himself. No works indeed
That ask robust tough sinews bred to toil,   405

Servile employ – but such as may amuse,
Not tire, demanding rather skill than force.
Proud of his well-spread walls, he views his trees
That meet (no barren interval between)
With pleasure more than ev'n their fruits afford,   410
Which, save himself who trains them, none can feel.
These, therefore, are his own peculiar charge;
No meaner hand may discipline the shoots,
None but his steel approach them. What is weak,
Distemper'd, or has lost prolific powers   415
Impair'd by age, his unrelenting hand
Dooms to the knife. Nor does he spare the soft
And succulent that feeds its giant growth
But barren, at th' expense of neighb'ring twigs
Less ostentatious, and yet studded thick   420
With hopeful gems. The rest, no portion left
That may disgrace his art, or disappoint
Large expectation, he disposes neat
At measur'd distances, that air and sun,
Admitted freely, may afford their aid,   425
And ventilate and warm the swelling buds.
Hence summer has her riches, autumn hence,
And hence ev'n winter fills his wither'd hand
With blushing fruits, and plenty not his own.
Fair recompense of labour well bestow'd,   430
And wise precaution, which a clime so rude
Makes needful still, whose spring is but the child
Of churlish winter, in her froward moods
Discov'ring much the temper of her sire.
For oft, as if in her the stream of mild   435
Maternal nature had reversed its course,
She brings her infants forth with many smiles,
But once deliver'd, kills them with a frown.
He, therefore, timely warn'd, himself supplies
Her want of care, screening and keeping warm   440
The plenteous bloom, that no rough blast may sweep
His garlands from the boughs. Again, as oft
As the sun peeps and vernal airs breathe mild,
The fence withdrawn, he gives them ev'ry beam,
And spreads his hopes before the blaze of day.   445

To raise the prickly and green-coated gourd
So grateful to the palate, and when rare
So coveted, else base and disesteem'd –
Food for the vulgar merely – is an art
That toiling ages have but just matur'd,   450
And at this moment unessay'd in song.
Yet gnats have had, and frogs and mice long since,
Their eulogy; those sang the Mantuan bard,
And these the Grecian, in ennobling strains;
And in thy numbers, Phillips, shines for aye   455
The solitary shilling. Pardon then,
Ye sage dispensers of poetic fame,
Th' ambition of one meaner far, whose pow'rs
Presuming an attempt not less sublime,
Pant for the praise of dressing to the taste   460
Of critic appetite, no sordid fare,
A cucumber, while costly yet and scarce.
    The stable yields a stercoraceous heap
Impregnated with quick fermenting salts,
And potent to resist the freezing blast.   465
For ere the beech and elm have cast their leaf
Deciduous, and when now November dark
Checks vegetation in the torpid plant
Expos'd to his cold breath, the task begins.
Warily, therefore, and with prudent heed   470
He seeks a favour'd spot, that where he builds
Th' agglomerated pile, his frame may front
The sun's meridian disk, and at the back
Enjoy close shelter, wall, or reeds, or hedge
Impervious to the wind. First he bids spread   475
Dry fern or litter'd hay, that may imbibe
Th' ascending damps; then leisurely impose
And lightly, shaking it with agile hand
From the full fork, the saturated straw.
What longest binds the closest, forms secure   480
The shapely side, that as it rises takes
By just degrees an overhanging breadth,
Shelt'ring the base with its projected eaves.
Th' uplifted frame, compact at every joint,

And overlaid with clear translucent glass,   485
He settles next upon the sloping mount,
Whose sharp declivity shoots off secure
From the dash'd pane the deluge as it falls.
He shuts it close, and the first labour ends.
Thrice must the voluble and restless earth   490
Spin round upon her axle, ere the warmth
Slow gathering in the midst, through the square mass
Diffus'd, attain the surface. When, behold!
A pestilent and most corrosive steam,
Like a gross fog Bœotian, rising fast,   495
And fast condens'd upon the dewy sash,
Asks egress; which obtain'd, the overcharg'd
And drench'd conservatory breathes abroad,
In volumes wheeling slow, the vapour dank,
And purified, rejoices to have lost   500
Its foul inhabitant. But to assuage
Th' impatient fervour which it first conceives
Within its reeking bosom, threat'ning death
To his young hopes, requires discreet delay.
Experience, slow preceptress, teaching oft   505
The way to glory by miscarriage foul,
Must prompt him, and admonish how to catch
Th' auspicious moment, when the temper'd heat,
Friendly to vital motion, may afford
Soft fomentation, and invite the seed.   510
The seed, selected wisely, plump and smooth
And glossy, he commits to pots of size
Diminutive, well fill'd with well-prepared
And fruitful soil, that has been treasur'd long,
And drunk no moisture from the dripping clouds.   515
These on the warm and genial earth that hides
The smoking manure and o'erspreads it all,
He places lightly, and as time subdues
The rage of fermentation, plunges deep
In the soft medium, till they stand immers'd.   520
Then rise the tender germs, upstarting quick,
And spreading wide their spongy lobes; at first
Pale, wan, and livid but assuming soon,

If fann'd by balmy and nutritious air,
Strain'd through the friendly mats, a vivid green.   525
Two leaves produc'd, two rough indented leaves,
Cautious he pinches from the second stalk
A pimple, that portends a future sprout,
And interdicts its growth. Thence straight succeed
The branches, sturdy to his utmost wish,   530
Prolific all, and harbingers of more.
The crowded roots demand enlargement now
And transplantation in an ampler space.
Indulg'd in what they wish, they soon supply
Large foliage, overshadowing golden flow'rs,   535
Blown on the summit of th' apparent fruit.
These have their sexes; and when summer shines,
The bee transports the fertilizing meal
From flow'r to flow'r, and even the breathing air
Wafts the rich prize to its appointed use.   540
Not so when winter scowls. Assistant art
Then acts in nature's office, brings to pass
The glad espousals and ensures the crop.

    Oh blest seclusion from a jarring world,   675
Which he thus occupied, enjoys! Retreat
Cannot indeed to guilty man restore
Lost innocence, or cancel follies past;
But it has peace, and much secures the mind
From all assaults of evil; proving still   680
A faithful barrier, not o'erleap'd with ease
By vicious custom, raging uncontroll'd
Abroad, and desolating public life.
When fierce temptation, seconded within
By traitor appetite, and arm'd with darts   685
Temper'd in hell, invades the throbbing breast,
To combat may be glorious, and success
Perhaps may crown us; but to fly is safe.
Had I the choice of sublunary good,
What could I wish, that I possess not here?   690
Health, leisure, means t' improve it, friendship, peace;
No loose or wanton, though a wandering muse,

And constant occupation without care.

Mansions once
Knew their own masters; and laborious hinds
That had surviv'd the father, serv'd the son.
Now the legitimate and rightful lord
Is but a transient guest, newly arriv'd   750
And soon to be supplanted. He that saw
His patrimonial timber cast its leaf,
Sells the last scantling, and transfers the price
To some shrewd sharper, ere it buds again.
Estates are landscapes, gaz'd upon awhile,   755
Then advertis'd, and auctioneer'd away.
The country starves, and they that feed th' o'ercharg'd
And surfeited lewd town with her fair dues,
By a just judgment strip and starve themselves.
The wings that waft our riches out of sight   760
Grow on the gamester's elbows; and th' alert
And nimble motion of those restless joints
That never tire, soon fans them all away.
Improvement too, the idol of the age,
Is fed with many a victim. Lo! he comes –   765
The omnipotent magician, Brown, appears.
Down falls the venerable pile, th' abode
Of our forefathers, a grave whisker'd race,
But tasteless. Springs a palace in its stead,
But in a distant spot; where more expos'd   770
It may enjoy th' advantage of the north
And agueish east, till time shall have transform'd
Those naked acres to a shelt'ring grove.
He speaks. The lake in front becomes a lawn,
Woods vanish, hills subside, and valleys rise;   775
And streams, as if created for his use,
Pursue the track of his directing wand,
Sinuous or straight, now rapid and now slow,
Now murm'ring soft, now roaring in cascades –
Even as he bids. The enraptured owner smiles.   780
'Tis finish'd! And yet finish'd as it seems,
Still wants a grace, the loveliest it could show,

A mine to satisfy th' enormous cost.
Drain'd to the last poor item of his wealth,
He sighs, departs, and leaves the accomplish'd plan   785
That he has touch'd, retouch'd, many a long day
Labour'd, and many a night pursu'd in dreams,
Just when it meets his hopes, and proves the heav'n
He wanted, for a wealthier to enjoy.

   Oh thou resort and mart of all the earth,   835
Checquer'd with all complexions of mankind,
And spotted with all crimes; in whom I see
Much that I love, and more that I admire,
And all that I abhor; thou freckled fair
That pleases and yet shocks me, I can laugh   840
And I can weep, can hope, and can despond,
Feel wrath and pity, when I think on thee!
Ten righteous would have saved a city once,
And thou hast many righteous – Well for thee –
That salt preserves thee; more corrupted else,   845
And therefore more obnoxious at this hour,
Than Sodom in her day had pow'r to be,
For whom God heard his Abr'am plead in vain.

from **Book IV: The Winter Evening**

Hark! 'tis the twanging horn! o'er yonder bridge,
That with its wearisome but needful length
Bestrides the wintry flood, in which the moon
Sees her unwrinkled face reflected bright –
He comes, the herald of a noisy world.   5
With spatter'd boots, strapp'd waist, and frozen locks,
News from all nations lumb'ring at his back.
True to his charge, the close-pack'd load behind,
Yet careless what he brings, his one concern
Is to conduct it to the destin'd inn,   10

And, having dropp'd the expected bag – pass on.
He whistles as he goes, light-hearted wretch,
Cold and yet cheerful: messenger of grief
Perhaps to thousands, and of joy to some;
To him indiff'rent whether grief or joy.   15
Houses in ashes, and the fall of stocks,
Births, deaths, and marriages, epistles wet
With tears, that trickled down the writer's cheeks
Fast as the periods from the fluent quill,
Or charg'd with am'rous sighs of absent swains   20
Or nymphs responsive, equally affect
His horse and him, unconscious of them all.
But oh th' important budget! usher'd in
With such heart-shaking music, who can say
What are its tidings? have our troops awak'd?   25
Or do they still, as if with opium drugg'd,
Snore to the murmurs of th' Atlantic wave?
Is India free? and does she wear her plum'd
And jewell'd turban with a smile of peace,
Or do we grind her still? The grand debate,   30
The popular harangue, the tart reply,
The logic, and the wisdom and the wit
And the fond laugh – I long to know them all;
I burn to set the imprison'd wranglers free,
And give them voice and utt'rance once again.   35
     Now stir the fire, and close the shutters fast,
Let fall the curtains, wheel the sofa round,
And, while the bubbling and loud-hissing urn
Throws up a steamy column, and the cups
That cheer but not inebriate, wait on each,   40
So let us welcome peaceful ev'ning in.
Not such his ev'ning, who with shining face
Sweats in the crowded theatre, and squeezed
And bor'd with elbow-points through both his sides,
Out-scolds the ranting actor on the stage.   45
Nor his, who patient stands till his feet throb,
And his head thumps, to feed upon the breath
Of patriots, bursting with heroic rage,
Or placemen, all tranquillity and smiles.

This folio of four pages, happy work!   50
Which not even critics criticise; that holds
Inquisitive attention while I read
Fast bound in chains of silence, which the fair,
Though eloquent themselves, yet fear to break;
What is it but a map of busy life,   55
Its fluctuations and its vast concerns?

  'Tis pleasant through the loop-holes of retreat
To peep at such a world: to see the stir
Of the great Babel and not feel the crowd: 90
To hear the roar she sends through all her gates
At a safe distance, where the dying sound
Falls a soft murmur on th' uninjur'd ear.
Thus sitting and surveying thus at ease,
The globe and its concerns, I seem advanc'd   95
To some secure and more than mortal height,
That lib'rates and exempts me from them all.
It turns submitted to my view, turns round
With all its generations; I behold
The tumult, and am still. The sound of war   100
Has lost its terrors ere it reaches me;
Grieves but alarms me not. I mourn the pride
And av'rice that make man a wolf to man;
Hear the faint echo of those brazen throats
By which he speaks the language of his heart,   105
And sigh, but never tremble at the sound.
He travels and expatiates, as the bee
From flow'r to flow'r, so he from land to land;
The manners, customs, policy of all
Pay contribution to the store he gleans;   110
He sucks intelligence in ev'ry clime,
And spreads the honey of his deep research
At his return – a rich repast for me.
He travels, and I too. I tread his deck,
Ascend his topmast, through his peering eyes   115
Discover countries, with a kindred heart
Suffer his woes, and share in his escapes,
While fancy, like the finger of a clock,
Runs the great circuit, and is still at home.

Fast falls a fleecy show'r. The downy flakes
Descending, and with never-ceasing lapse
Softly alighting upon all below,
Assimilate all objects. Earth receives
Gladly the thick'ning mantle, and the green   330
And tender blade that fear'd the chilling blast,
Escapes unhurt beneath so warm a veil.
    In such a world, so thorny, and where none
Finds happiness unblighted, or if found,
Without some thistly sorrow at its side,   335
It seems the part of wisdom, and no sin
Against the law of love to measure lots
With less distinguish'd than ourselves, that thus
We may with patience bear our mod'rate ills,
And sympathize with others, suff'ring more.   340
Ill fares the trav'ller now, and he that stalks
In pond'rous boots beside his reeking team.
The wain goes heavily, impeded sore
By congregated loads adhering close
To the clogg'd wheels; and in its sluggish pace,   345
Noiseless, appears a moving hill of snow.
The toiling steeds expand the nostril wide,
While ev'ry breath by respiration strong
Forc'd downward, is consolidated soon
Upon their jutting chests. He, form'd to bear   350
The pelting brunt of the tempestuous night,
With half-shut eyes, and pucker'd cheeks, and teeth
Presented bare against the storm, plods on.
One hand secures his hat, save when with both
He brandishes his pliant length of whip,   355
Resounding oft, and never heard in vain.
Oh happy! and in my account, denied
That sensibility of pain with which
Refinement is endued, thrice happy thou.
Thy frame, robust and hardy, feels indeed   360
The piercing cold, but feels it unimpair'd.
The learned finger never need explore
Thy vig'rous pulse; and the unhealthful east,

That breathes the spleen, and searches ev'ry bone
Of the infirm, is wholesome air to thee.   365
Thy days roll on, exempt from household care;
Thy waggon is thy wife; and the poor beasts,
That drag the dull companion to and fro,
Thine helpless charge, dependent on thy care.
Ah treat them kindly! rude as thou appear'st   370
Yet show that thou hast mercy, which the great
With needless hurry whirl'd from place to place,
Humane as they would seem, not always show.

No. We are polish'd now! The rural lass,
Whom once her virgin modesty and grace,   535
Her artless manners and her neat attire,
So dignified, that she was hardly less
Than the fair shepherdess of old romance,
Is seen no more. The character is lost.
Her head, adorn'd with lappets pinn'd aloft,   540
And ribands streaming gay, superbly rais'd
And magnified beyond all human size,
Indebted to some smart wig-weaver's hand
For more than half the tresses it sustains;
Her elbows ruffled, and her tott'ring form   545
Ill propp'd upon French heels; she might be deemed
(But that the basket dangling on her arm
Interprets her more truly,) of a rank
Too proud for dairy work or sale of eggs.
Expect her soon with footboy at her heels,   550
No longer blushing for her awkward load,
Her train and her umbrella all her care.
   The town has ting'd the country. And the stain
Appears a spot upon a vestal's robe,
The worse for what it soils. The fashion runs   555
Down into scenes still rural, but alas!
Scenes rarely grac'd with rural manners now.
Time was when in the pastoral retreat
Th' unguarded door was safe. Men did not watch
T' invade another's right, or guard their own.   560
Then sleep was undisturb'd by fear, unscar'd
By drunken howlings; and the chilling tale

Of midnight murder was a wonder heard
With doubtful credit, told to frighten babes.
But farewell now to unsuspicious nights   565
And slumbers unalarm'd. Now, ere you sleep,
See that your polish'd arms be primed with care,
And drop the night-bolt. Ruffians are abroad.

from Book V: The Winter Morning Walk

'Tis morning; and the sun with ruddy orb
Ascending fires the horizon: while the clouds
That crowd away before the driving wind,
More ardent as the disk emerges more,
Resemble most some city in a blaze,   5
Seen through the leafless wood. His slanting ray
Slides ineffectual down the snowy vale,
And tinging all with his own rosy hue,
From ev'ry herb and ev'ry spiry blade
Stretches a length of shadow o'er the field.   10
Mine, spindling into longitude immense,
In spite of gravity and sage remark
That I myself am but a fleeting shade,
Provokes me to a smile. With eye askance
I view the muscular proportion'd limb   15
Transform'd to a lean shank. The shapeless pair,
As they design'd to mock me, at my side
Take step for step; and, as I near approach
The cottage, walk along the plaster'd wall,
Preposterous sight! the legs without the man.   20
The verdure of the plain lies buried deep
Beneath the dazzling deluge; and the bents
And coarser grass, upspearing o'er the rest,
Of late unsightly and unseen, now shine
Conspicuous, and, in bright apparel clad   25
And fledg'd with icy feathers, nod superb.
The cattle mourn in corners where the fence

Screens them, and seem half petrified to sleep
In unrecumbent sadness. There they wait
Their wonted fodder; not like hung'ring man,   30
Fretful if unsupplied, but silent, meek,
And patient of the slow-pac'd swain's delay.
He from the stack carves out the accustom'd load,
Deep-plunging, and again deep-plunging oft
His broad keen knife into the solid mass.   35
Smooth as a wall the upright remnant stands,
With such undeviating and even force
He severs it away: no needless care,
Lest storms should overset the leaning pile
Deciduous, or its own unbalanc'd weight.   40
Forth goes the woodman, leaving unconcern'd
The cheerful haunts of man, to wield the axe
And drive the wedge, in yonder forest drear,
From morn to eve his solitary task.
Shaggy, and lean and shrewd, with pointed ears   45
And tail cropp'd short, half lurcher and half cur –
His dog attends him. Close behind his heel
Now creeps he slow; and now with many a frisk
Wide-scamp'ring snatches up the drifted snow
With iv'ry teeth, or ploughs it with his snout;   50
Then shakes his powder'd coat and barks for joy.
Heedless of all his pranks, the sturdy churl
Moves right toward the mark; nor stops for aught,
But now and then with pressure of his thumb
T' adjust the fragrant charge of a short tube   55
That fumes beneath his nose: the trailing cloud
Streams far behind him, scenting all the air.
Now from the roost or from the neighb'ring pale,
Where diligent to catch the first faint gleam
Of smiling day, they gossip'd side by side,   60
Come trooping at the housewife's well-known call
The feather'd tribes domestic. Half on wing,
And half on foot, they brush the fleecy flood,
Conscious, and fearful of too deep a plunge.
The sparrows peep, and quit the shelt'ring eaves   65
To seize the fair occasion. Well they eye
The scatter'd grain, and thievishly resolv'd

T' escape th' impending famine, often scar'd
As oft return, a pert voracious kind.
Clean riddance quickly made, one only care   70
Remains to each, the search of sunny nook,
Or shed impervious to the blast. Resign'd
To sad necessity the cock foregoes
His wonted strut, and, wading at their head
With well-consider'd steps, seems to resent   75
His alter'd gait and stateliness retrench'd.
How find the myriads that in summer cheer
The hills and vallies with their ceaseless songs,
Due sustenance, or where subsist they now?
Earth yields them nought: th' imprison'd worm is safe   80
Beneath the frozen clod; all seeds of herbs
Lie cover'd close, and berry-bearing thorns
That feed the thrush (whatever some suppose)
Afford the smaller minstrels no supply.
The long protracted rigour of the year   85
Thins all their num'rous flocks. In chinks and holes
Ten thousand seek an unmolested end
As instinct prompts, self-buried ere they die.
The very rooks and daws forsake the fields,
Where neither grub, nor root, nor earth-nut, now   90
Repays their labour more; and perch'd aloft
By the way-side, or stalking in the path,
Lean pensioners upon the traveller's track,
Pick up their nauseous dole, though sweet to them,
Of voided pulse or half digested grain.   95
The streams are lost amid the splendid blank
O'erwhelming all distinction. On the flood,
Indurated and fixt, the snowy weight
Lies undissolv'd, while silently beneath
And unperceiv'd, the current steals away.   100
Not so, where scornful of a check it leaps
The mill-dam, dashes on the restless wheel,
And wantons in the pebbly gulf below.
No frost can bind it there. Its utmost force
Can but arrest the light and smoky mist   105
That in its fall the liquid sheet throws wide.
And see where it has hung the embroider'd banks

With forms so various, that no pow'rs of art,
The pencil or the pen, may trace the scene!
Here glitt'ring turrets rise, upbearing high 110
(Fantastic misarrangement) on the roof
Large growth of what may seem the sparkling trees
And shrubs of fairy land. The chrystal drops
That trickle down the branches, fast congeal'd,
Shoot into pillars of pellucid length, 115
And prop the pile they but adorn'd before.
Here grotto within grotto safe defies
The sun-beam. There emboss'd and fretted wild,
The growing wonder takes a thousand shapes
Capricious, in which fancy seeks in vain 120
The likeness of some object seen before.
Thus nature works as if to mock at art,
And in defiance of her rival pow'rs;
By these fortuitous and random strokes
Performing such inimitable feats 125
As she with all her rules can never reach.
Less worthy of applause, though more admired,
Because a novelty, the work of man,
Imperial mistress of the fur-clad Russ!
Thy most magnificent and mighty freak, 130
The wonder of the north. No forest fell
When thou wouldst build; no quarry sent its stores
T' enrich thy walls: but thou didst hew the floods,
And make thy marble of the glassy wave.
In such a palace Aristæus found 135
Cyrene, when he bore the plaintive tale
Of his lost bees to her maternal ear.
In such a palace poetry might place
The armoury of winter, where his troops
The gloomy clouds find weapons, arrowy sleet, 140
Skin-piercing volley, blossom-bruising hail,
And snow that often blinds the traveller's course,
And wraps him in an unsuspected tomb.
Silently as a dream the fabric rose.
No sound of hammer or of saw was there. 145
Ice upon ice, the well-adjusted parts
Were soon conjoin'd, nor other cement ask'd

Than water interfused to make them one.
Lamps gracefully dispos'd and of all hues
Illumined ev'ry side. A wat'ry light   150
Gleam'd through the clear transparency, that seem'd
Another moon new-risen, or meteor fall'n
From heaven to earth, of lambent flame serene.
So stood the brittle prodigy; though smooth
And slipp'ry the materials, yet frost-bound   155
Firm as a rock.

    Then shame to manhood, and opprobious more
To France, than all her losses and defeats   380
Old or of later date, by sea or land,
Her house of bondage worse than that of old
Which God aveng'd on Pharaoh – the Bastile!
Ye horrid tow'rs, the abode of broken hearts;
Ye dungeons and ye cages of despair,   385
That monarchs have supplied from age to age
With music such as suits their sovereign ears –
The sighs and groans of miserable men!
There's not an English heart that would not leap
To hear that ye were fall'n at last; to know   390
That ev'n our enemies, so oft employ'd
In forging chains for us, themselves were free.
For he that values liberty, confines
His zeal for her predominance within
No narrow bounds; her cause engages him   395
Wherever pleaded.

from **Book VI: The Winter Walk at Noon**

    The night was winter in his roughest mood;
The morning sharp and clear. But now at noon
Upon the southern side of the slant hills,
And where the woods fence off the northern blast,   60
The season smiles, resigning all its rage,

And has the warmth of May. The vault is blue
Without a cloud, and white without a speck
The dazzling splendour of the scene below.
Again the harmony comes o'er the vale;   65
And through the trees I view th' embattled tow'r
Whence all the music. I again perceive
The soothing influence of the wafted strains,
And settle in soft musings as I tread
The walk still verdant under oaks and elms,   70
Whose outspread branches overarch the glade.
The roof, though moveable through all its length
As the wind sways it, has yet well suffic'd,
And intercepting in their silent fall
The frequent flakes, has kept a path for me.   75
No noise is here, or none that hinders thought.
The redbreast warbles still, but is content
With slender notes, and more than half suppress'd.
Pleas'd with his solitude, and flitting light
From spray to spray, where'er he rests he shakes   80
From many a twig the pendent drops of ice,
That tinkle in the wither'd leaves below.
Stillness acompanied with sounds so soft
Charms more than silence.

Where now the vital energy that mov'd,
While summer was, the pure and subtle lymph   135
Through th' imperceptible meand'ring veins
Of leaf and flow'r? It sleeps; and th' icy touch
Of unprolific winter has impress'd
A cold stagnation on th' intestine tide.
But let the months go round, a few short months,   140
And all shall be restored. These naked shoots,
Barren as lances, among which the wind
Makes wintry music, sighing as it goes,
Shall put their graceful foliage on again,
And, more aspiring, and with ampler spread,   145
Shall boast new charms, and more than they have lost.
Then, each in its peculiar honours clad,
Shall publish even to the distant eye,
Its family and tribe. Laburnum rich

In streaming gold; syringa iv'ry pure;   150
The scented and the scentless rose; this red
And of an humbler growth, the other tall,
And throwing up into the darkest gloom
Of neighb'ring cypress or more sable yew,
Her silver globes, light as the foamy surf   155
That the wind severs from the broken wave.
The lilac various in array, now white,
Now sanguine, and her beauteous head now set
With purple spikes pyramidal, as if,
Studious of ornament, yet unresolved   160
Which hue she most approv'd, she chose them all.
Copious of flow'rs the woodbine, pale and wan,
But well compensating her sickly looks
With never-cloying odours, early and late.
Hypericum, all bloom, so thick a swarm   165
Of flow'rs like flies clothing her slender rods
That scarce a leaf appears. Mezerion too,
Though leafless, well attir'd, and thick beset
With blushing wreaths investing ev'ry spray.
Althæa with the purple eye; the broom,   170
Yellow and bright as bullion unalloy'd,
Her blossoms; and luxuriant above all
The jasmine, throwing wide her elegant sweets,
The deep dark green of whose unvarnish'd leaf
Makes more conspicuous, and illumines more   175
The bright profusion of her scatter'd stars.
These have been, and these shall be in their day;
And all this uniform, uncolour'd scene,
Shall be dismantled of its fleecy load,
And flush into variety again.   180
From dearth to plenty, and from death to life,
Is Nature's progress when she lectures man
In heavenly truth; evincing, as she makes
The grand transition, that there lives and works
A soul in all things, and that soul is God.   185

The Lord of all, himself through all diffus'd,
Sustains, and is the life of all that lives.
Nature is but a name for an effect,

Whose cause is God. He feeds the secret fire
By which the mighty process is maintain'd,   225
Who sleeps not, is not weary; in whose sight
Slow-circling ages are as transient days;
Whose work is without labour; whose designs
No flaw deforms, no difficulty thwarts;
And whose beneficence no charge exhausts.   230
Him blind antiquity profan'd, not serv'd,
With self-taught rites and under various names,
Female and male, Pomona, Pales, Pan,
And Flora and Vertumnus; peopling earth
With tutelary goddesses and gods   235
That were not; and commending, as they would,
To each some province, garden, field, or grove.
But all are under one. One spirit – His
Who wore the platted thorns with bleeding brows –
Rules universal nature. Not a flow'r   240
But shows some touch in freckle, streak or stain,
Of his unrivall'd pencil. He inspires
Their balmy odours and imparts their hues,
And bathes their eyes with nectar, and includes
In grains as countless as the sea-side sands,   245
The forms with which he sprinkles all the earth.
Happy who walks with him! whom what he finds
Of flavour or of scent in fruit or flow'r,
Or what he views of beautiful or grand
In Nature, from the broad majestic oak   250
To the green blade that twinkles in the sun,
Prompts with remembrance of a present God.

   Here, unmolested, through whatever sign   295
The sun proceeds, I wander. Neither mist,
Nor freezing sky, nor sultry, checking me,
Nor stranger intermeddling with my joy.
Ev'n in the spring and play-time of the year
That calls th' unwonted villager abroad   300
With all her little ones, a sportive train,
To gather king-cups in the yellow mead,
And prink their hair with daisies, or to pick
A cheap but wholesome sallad from the brook,

These shades are all my own. The tim'rous hare,   305
Grown so familiar with her frequent guest,
Scarce shuns me; and the stock-dove, unalarm'd
Sits cooing in the pine-tree, nor suspends
His long love-ditty for my near approach.
Drawn from his refuge in some lonely elm   310
That age or injury has hollow'd deep,
Where on his bed of wool and matted leaves,
He has outslept the winter, ventures forth
To frisk awhile, and bask in the warm sun,
The squirrel, flippant, pert, and full of play.   315
He sees me, and at once, swift as a bird,
Ascends the neighb'ring beech; there whisks his brush,
And perks his ears, and stamps and scolds aloud,
With all the prettiness of feign'd alarm,
And anger insignificantly fierce.   320
    The heart is hard in nature, and unfit
For human fellowship, as being void
Of sympathy, and therefore dead alike
To love and friendship both, that is not pleas'd
With sight of animals enjoying life,   325
Nor feels their happiness augment his own.
The bounding fawn, that darts across the glade
When none pursues, through mere delight of heart,
And spirits buoyant with excess of glee;
The horse as wanton, and almost as fleet,   330
That skims the spacious meadow at full speed,
Then stops and snorts, and throwing high his heels,
Starts to the voluntary race again;
The very kine that gambol at high noon,
The total herd receiving first from one   335
That leads the dance, a summons to be gay,
Though wild their strange vagaries, and uncouth
Their efforts, yet resolv'd with one consent
To give such act and utt'rance as they may
To ecstasy too big to be suppress'd —   340
These, and a thousand images of bliss,
With which kind nature graces ev'ry scene
Where cruel man defeats not her design,
Impart to the benevolent, who wish

All that are capable of pleasure pleas'd,   345
A far superior happiness to theirs,
The comfort of a reasonable joy.
   Man scarce had ris'n, obedient to his call
Who form'd him, from the dust his future grave,
When he was crown'd as never king was since.   350
God set the diadem upon his head,
And angel choirs attended. Wond'ring stood
The new-made monarch, while before him pass'd,
All happy, and all perfect in their kind,
The creatures, summon'd from their various haunts   355
To see their sovereign, and confess his sway.
Vast was his empire, absolute his pow'r,
Or bounded only by a law whose force
'Twas his sublimest privilege to feel
And own – the law of universal love.   360
He rul'd with meekness, they obey'd with joy.
No cruel purpose lurk'd within his heart,
And no distrust of his intent in theirs.
So Eden was a scene of harmless sport,
Where kindness on his part who rul'd the whole   365
Begat a tranquil confidence in all,
And fear as yet was not, nor cause for fear.
But sin marr'd all; and the revolt of man,
That source of evils not exhausted yet,
Was punish'd with revolt of his from him.   370
Garden of God, how terrible the change
Thy groves and lawns then witness'd! Ev'ry heart,
Each animal of ev'ry name, conceiv'd
A jealousy and an instinctive fear,
And conscious of some danger, either fled   375
Precipitate the loath'd abode of man,
Or growl'd defiance in such angry sort,
As taught him, too, to tremble in his turn.
Thus harmony and family accord
Were driv'n from Paradise; and in that hour   380
The seeds of cruelty that since have swell'd
To such gigantic and enormous growth,
Were sown in human nature's fruitful soil.
Hence date the persecution and the pain

That man inflicts on all inferior kinds,   385
Regardless of their plaints. To make him sport,
To gratify the frenzy of his wrath,
Or his base gluttony, are causes good
And just, in his account, why bird and beast
Should suffer torture, and the streams be dyed   390
With blood of their inhabitants impal'd.
Earth groans beneath the burthen of a war
Wag'd with defenceless innocence, while he,
Not satisfied to prey on all around,
Adds tenfold bitterness to death, by pangs   395
Needless, and first torments ere he devours.
Now happiest they that occupy the scenes
The most remote from his abhorr'd resort,
Whom once, as delegate of God on earth,
They fear'd, and, as his perfect image, loved.   400
The wilderness is theirs with all its caves,
Its hollow glens, its thickets, and its plains,
Unvisited by man. There they are free,
And howl and roar as likes them, uncontrol'd,
Nor ask his leave to slumber or to play.   405
Woe to the tyrant if he dare intrude
Within the confines of their wild domain;
The lion tells him – I am monarch here –
And if he spares him, spares him on the terms
Of royal mercy, and through gen'rous scorn   410
To rend a victim trembling at his foot.
In measure, as by force of instinct drawn,
Or by necessity constrain'd, they live
Dependent upon man; those in his fields,
These at his crib, and some beneath his roof.   415
They prove too often at how dear a rate
He sells protection. Witness at his foot,
The spaniel dying, for some venial fault,
Under dissection of the knotted scourge.
Witness the patient ox, with stripes and yells   420
Driv'n to the slaughter, goaded, as he runs
To madness, while the savage at his heels
Laughs at the frantic sufferer's fury, spent
Upon the guiltless passenger o'erthrown.

He too is witness, noblest of the train 425
That wait on man, the flight-performing horse:
With unsuspecting readiness he takes
His murd'rer on his back, and push'd all day,
With bleeding sides and flanks that heave for life,
To the far-distant goal, arrives and dies. 430
So little mercy shows who needs so much!

   I would not enter on my list of friends 560
(Though grac'd with polish'd manners and fine sense,
Yet wanting sensibility) the man
Who needlessly sets foot upon a worm.
An inadvertent step may crush the snail
That crawls at ev'ning in the public path, 565
But he that has humanity, forewarn'd,
Will tread aside, and let the reptile live.

So life glides smoothly and by stealth away, 995
More golden than that age of fabled gold
Renown'd in ancient song; not vex'd with care
Or stain'd with guilt, beneficent, approv'd
Of God and man, and peaceful in its end.
So glide my life away! and so at last, 1000
My share of duties decently fulfill'd,
May some disease, not tardy to perform
Its destin'd office, yet with gentle stroke,
Dismiss me, weary, to a safe retreat,
Beneath the turf that I have often trod. 1005

Notes

The text follows *Poems, by William Cowper, of the Inner Temple, Esq. in Two Volumes,* ed. Joseph Johnson (1800), with reference also to *The Poems of William Cowper* (Vol. I, 1980; Vols. II and II, 1985), ed. John D. Baird and Charles Ryskamp and to *The Poetical Works of William Cowper,* ed. H.S. Milford, revised by Norma Russell (1967).

Lines written During a Period of Insanity (once assigned to 1763, more probably written 1774; published in *Memoirs,* 1816) **16 Abiram:** rebelled against Moses and Aaron.

The Castaway (written 1799; published 1803) The poem is based on an incident described in Richard Walter's *A Voyage Round the World . . . by George Anson* in which a sailor who had fallen overboard was left to drown as the ship was unable to put about. **3 destin'd wretch:** hints of Calvinist predestination. **7 chief:** Anson. **Albion:** Britain. **50 narrative:** ship's log.

Verses, Supposed to be Written by Alexander Selkirk (written ?; published 1782) Selkirk was marooned on the island of Juan Fernandez, off Chile, from October 1704 to February 1709, when he was rescued by Captain Woodes Rogers. Later, his story inspired Defoe's *Robinson Crusoe.*

On the Loss of the Royal George (written 1782–3; published 1803) During a refit in August 1782, the *Royal George,* flagship of Admiral Kempenfelt, was heeled over by running the starboard guns to the port side. At this point, the decayed timbers cracked, and the ship went down with 800 people on board. **14 Kempenfelt:** Richard (1718–82), who had captured twenty ships from the French in the previous December at Ushant. **25 Weigh:** raise.

The Shrubbery (written 1773; published 1782) In happier times (*c.* 1784), Cowper wrote an inscription for the Moss House in the shrubbery, which celebrated the tranquillity and peace of mind that he enjoyed in such seclusion.

Yardley Oak (written 1792; published 1804) The tree stood in Yardley Chase, near Olney. **5 excoriate:** with peeling bark, **deform:** disfigured. **10 Druids:** the oak was believed to be sacred to the Druids. **11–16:** a benighted time, before Christ's redemption of mankind. **25 Design'd:** to be 'thy cradle'. **26 dibbling the glebe:** sowing the soil. **30 searce:** sieve. **35 Twins:** Castor and Pollux, sired on Leda by Zeus, disguised as a swan. **36 stars:** constellation Gemini. **41 Dodona:** Greek oracle where prophecies were delivered from oak groves. **53 champain:** open countryside. **54 cope:** canopy. **66 wens globose:** spherical lump, excrescence. **89 declension:** decline. **94 bole:** trunk. **96 flagg'd admiral:** admiral's flagship (as the *Royal George*.) **99 knee-timber:** crooked branches of the oak used for angled ship's timbers. **101–3** the exploitation of woodland to raise money for political campaigning. **110 Embowell'd:** disembowelled. **116 sincere:** sound. **123 Pulveriz'd of venality:** ground to dust by corruption. **145 bourn:** destination. **152 Jacob:** see Genesis 47:9. **154 Prediluvian:** living before the Flood. **156–60** borrowed from his own translation of the *Iliad* VI, 175ff (Cowper's note in MS). **162 Maeonian:** Homer was supposedly a native of Maeonia in Asia Minor. **167 man:** Adam. **184** poem appears to be unfinished.

The Poplar Field (written 1784; published 1800) The field, to the west of Lavendon Mill, was a mile and a half from Cowper's house. There is a description in his letter to Lady Hesketh of 1 May 1786.

The Diverting History of John Gilpin (written and published 1782) First published anonymously in *The Public Advertiser* of November 1782, the poem immediately became a vogue. There were chapbook versions sold in the street; recitations; 'sequels'; and prints. **3 train-band:** citizen's militia. **eke:** also. **11 Bell at Edmonton:** inn at what was then a village in Middlesex, north of London. **23 calender:** a cloth worker who smoothed and glazed material. **49 saddle-tree:** framework of saddle. **59 Betty:** generic term for a maid. **97 neck or nought:** ready to take a risk. **115 carries weight:** extra weight, as in handicap races. **119 turnpikemen:** toll-gate attendants. **122 reeking:** steaming with heat. **135 wash:** a stream crossing the road. **152 Ware:** town in Hertfordshire, ten miles to the north of Edmonton. **162 trim:** condition. **178 merry pin:** good humour. **222 amain:** at speed.

The Colubriad (written 1782; published 1806) There is an account of this episode in Cowper's letter to William Unwin of 3 August 1782. **Title:**

from Latin 'coluber', a snake. **11 Count de Grasse:** admiral of the French fleet, and popular with English cartoonists who exaggerated his overly long wig. **19 Dutch hoe:** a thrust-hoe as opposed to a draw-hoe.

Epitaph on a Hare (written 1783; published in *The Gentleman's Magazine*, December 1784; *Poems*, 1800) Cowper placed a long account of his hares in *The Gentleman's Magazine*, June 1784; it subsequently supplied a footnote for *The Task*, III, 351. **3 tainted:** left a spoor. **8 Jack-hare:** the buck, or male. **10 pittance:** originally an allowance of food doled out by religious orders. **16 scour his maw:** clean out the stomach, aiding digestion. **18 pippins:** apples. **40 Puss:** another of Cowper's hares, on whose death (1786) he wrote a prose epitaph; see *The Task*, III, 334–51.

On the Death of Mrs Throckmorton's Bulfinch (written 1788; published in *The Gentleman's Magazine*, February 1789; *Poems*, 1795) For a similar mock-elegy, in the same form, see Thomas Gray's 'Ode on the Death of a Favourite Cat' (1748). **3 Maria:** Maria Catherine Giffard (1762–1821), married to John Throckmorton in 1782. The Throckmortons were friends of Cowper, allowing him the freedom of their estate at Weston Underwood. **7 Rhenus:** River Rhine, the bullfinch probably having been imported. **12 flagelet:** small wind-instrument. **16 Aurora:** goddess of the dawn. **62–3 Bacchanalians . . . Thracian Hebrus' side:** Orpheus, the legendary poet of Thrace, was torn to pieces by the female followers of Dionysus, and his head flung into the River Hebrus.

The Retired Cat (written 1791; published 1803) **16 watering pot:** now more usually, watering-can. **18 sedan:** closed chair carried by two bearers. **62 Sol:** sun.

To the Nightingale (written 1792; published 1803) **9 Philomel:** daughter of a king of Athens was transformed into a nightingale after her sister's husband had raped her and cut out her tongue.

On a Spaniel called Beau (written 1793; published 1803)

Beau's Reply (written 1793; published 1803)

The Negro's Complaint (written 1788; published in *Stuart's Star*, 1789; *Poems*, 1800) The poem was taken up by the abolitionists and published widely. **22 jovial:** convivial. **24 cane:** sugar-cane.

Pity for Poor Africans (written 1788; published in *Northampton Mercury*, August 1788; *Poems*, 1800) **epigraph: Video** . . . 'I see the better course, and approve it; but I still follow the worse' (Ovid, *Metamorphoses*, vii, 20). **16 go snacks:** divide the profits. **19 out of my mint:** of my own invention.

The Morning Dream (written 1788; published in *The Gentleman's Magazine*, November 1788; *Poems*, 1800)

Sweet Meat Has Sour Sauce (written 1788; published 1837) **Title:** proverbial. **7 electrical knock:** referring to the fashion for electroconvulsive therapy. **10 regales:** choice refreshments. **14 supple-jack** and **rattan:** tropical plants used as canes. **20 comfits:** sugar plums, sweets. **44 Caesars and Pompeys:** common slave-names.

Olney Hymns (written 1771–2; published 1779) The Olney collection comprised sixty-six contributions by Cowper, and 282 by John Newton.

Light Shining Out of Darkness (written at the end of 1772, shortly before the breakdown of January 1773)

On the Receipt of my Mother's Picture (written 1790; published 1798) The portrait in question was a head-and-shoulders miniature by D. Heins. It was sent to Cowper by Anne Bodham, *née* Donne, who was his mother's niece. **19 Elysian:** blissfully happy, after Elysium where, in Greek mythology, the souls of the blessed dead were assigned. **21 when I learn'd:** Cowper was almost six when his mother died on 7 November 1737. **45 deplor'd:** grieved for. **53 past'ral house:** Berkhamsted Rectory. **88 Albion:** Britain. **99 long since:** Revd John Cowper died 1756.

To Mary (written 1792; published 1803) Mary Unwin suffered her second stroke in May of 1792. **1 twentieth year:** dating from the breakdown of January 1773. **46 wintry age:** in 1792 Mrs Unwin was sixty-eight.

From The Task (written October 1783 to September 1784; published 1785)

From the 'Advertisement': 'The history of the following production is briefly this:– A lady, fond of blank verse, demanded a poem of that kind from the author, and gave him the SOFA for a subject. He obeyed; and, having much leisure, connected another subject with it; and, pursuing the train of thought to which his situation and turn of mind led him, brought forth at length, instead of the trifle which he at first intended, a serious affair – a Volume!' Cowper's inspiration was Lady Ann Austen, a baronet's widow, whom he had met when she was visiting her sister near Olney in 1781. When she took up residence in Olney in 1782, she became a close companion of Cowper and Mary Unwin, and acted out the part of Cowper's 'muse'. As well as requesting a piece on 'the sofa', it was she who recounted the story of John Gilpin.

From Book I: The Sofa: 144 companion: Mrs Unwin. **145 this twentieth winter:** as Cowper had met Mrs Unwin late in 1765, the winter of 1783–4 was the nineteenth. Twentieth would, of course, have coincided with the date of submission to the publisher. **154 eminence:** between Olney and Weston Underwood. **167 elms:** according to an account in *Cowper Illustrated* (1803), these trees were, in fact, poplars. **173 square tow'r:** Clifton Reynes church. **174 Tall spire:** of Olney church. **200 one:** the nightingale. **203 sublime:** at a great height. **205 pie:** magpie. **boding:** proverbially, a bird of omens. **211 weather-house:** a model house which uses humidity levels to predict weather conditions. **221–5 the *peasant's nest*:** such a passage confirms Cowper's resistance to any form of romantic primitivism: cf. his attitude to gypsies, Bk I, 557–91.

278 alcove: 'A sexagon, of a light and graceful form, composed of wood', *Cowper Illustrated*. **288 clown:** simple countryman. **289 speculative height:** a vantage point that encourages contemplation. **298 boorish:** originally relating to a husbandman or peasant; hence, coarse. **311 umbrageous:** providing shade.

416 fictions of the loom: tapestries. **425 Italian light:** the vogue for painters of Italian scenes (Claude, Poussin, Salvator Rosa), which had been stimulated by the Grand Tour.

534–56 Crazy Kate: according to Cowper, in a letter to Joseph Hill, 24 May 1788, there was an original Kate. She looks forward to Wordsworth's rustic solitaries. **569 pedigree:** gypsies claim ancestry from the Egyptians. **588 rovers of the sylvan world:** the sudden intrusion of pastoral vocabulary may be prompted by Cowper's sneaking admiration for their 'natural' existence.

620 favour'd isles: Society Islands and Friendly Islands; now Tonga.
633 gentle savage: Omai was brought from the Society Islands to
England by Captain Furneaux in 1774. He was taken up by high society,
presented to George III, painted by Reynolds, and taken back to the South
Seas by Captain Cook in 1777. Within four years he had died.

755 sedans: closed chairs, carried by two bearers. **766 satellite:** the
moon.

From Book II: The Time-Piece Cowper explained the title to John
Newton: 'The book to which it belongs is intended to strike the hour that
gives notice of approaching judgement; and dealing pretty largely in the
signs of the *times*, seems to be denominated as it is with a sufficient degree of
accommodation to the subject' (11 December 1784). **2 boundless
contiguity:** unbroken extent. **4 war:** in the American colonies.
15 devotes: consigns to destruction. **16 frith:** arm of the sea, as the
English and French facing each other across the English Channel. **21–47:**
see Cowper's poems on slavery. In June 1783, the Quakers of England
petitioned parliament to forbid all traffic in slaves.

624 side-box station at half price: side-boxes were the most expensive
seats, but after the third act, prices halved. **628 tavern quill:** toothpick.
629 rout: fashionable assemblies. **643 contemns:** views with con-
tempt. **648 flambeaux:** torches. **652 hackney'd home unlackey'd:**
goes home in a hired carriage rather than in her own, attended by servants.
657 fortune's velvet altar: gaming table.

From Book III: The Garden 108–20: after his breakdown in 1763,
Cowper spent some eighteen months in Nathaniel Cotton's asylum at St
Alban's. It was here that he experienced an evangelical conversion, and,
when released, he retreated to take up residence with the Unwins.
113 archers: Cowper sees his 'enemies' and Christ's as being the same.
115 soliciting: drawing out. **139–49:** Cowper's comments in his letter
on modern historians are generally scathing (to Newton, 27 July 1783).
145 puzzled: confused. **150–4:** geologists were beginning to challenge
biblical chronology, perhaps the most prominent being Buffon. **159 plan-
etary:** moving. **172 fume:** smoke, and idle fantasy.

297 progenitor: Adam. **318 spleen:** depression of the spirits.
326 field: bloodsports. **334 hare:** Puss, see 'Epitaph on a Hare'.

351 one hare: a reference to John Gay's (1685–1732) 'The Hare and Many Friends' in his *Fables* (1727).

390 her: in Cowper's case, Mary Unwin. **391 lymph:** water, but here probably tea. **400 lubbard labour:** clumsy servants. **408 well-spread walls:** what follows is a description of trained fruit trees, dependent on the skill of the pruner; espaliers, fans, cordons etc. **421 gems:** buds. **440 screening:** sacking or matting hung to protect blossom from late frosts. **446–543:** this passage of horticultural instruction (together with hints on pruning) is a slightly arch genuflection to the manner of Virgil's *Georgics*. The Latin poet celebrated a fairly hard rural existence, full of practical agricultural advice, which has become miniaturised in *The Task* to a leisurely form of gentlemanly pursuit. **446 prickly and green-coated gourd:** short, prickly cucumbers were the best early crop. **446 grateful:** pleasant. **452 gnats:** reference to *Culex*, a mock-heroic poem on a shepherd saved from snake-bite by a gnat, once attributed to Virgil. **frogs and mice:** reference to *Batrachomyomachia*, a poem which parodies an epic encounter between frogs and mice; once attributed to Homer, it was translated by Cowper (1791). **453 Mantuan bard:** Virgil was born near Mantua. **455 Phillips:** John Philips (1676–1708), poet who wrote *The Splendid Shilling* (1703) and the georgical *Cider* (1706). **463 stercoraceous:** made up of dung. **472–3 front/the sun's meridian disk:** face the south. **477 impose:** deposit. **489 first labour:** comic echo of the labours of Hercules. **490 voluble:** rolling, spinning. **495 Bœotian:** Greek legend had it that the people of Bœotia were stupid from breathing in their dank atmosphere. **496 sash:** one of the lights of the **conservatory** (498) or coldframe. **499 volumes:** wreaths. **505 preceptress:** teacher. **510 fomentation:** warmth. **522 lobes:** leaf shoots. **523 livid:** blue-green. **527 pinches:** pinching out extra buds concentrates the plant's energy. **541 Assistant art:** manual fertilisation.

675–93 Feelings very close to these can be found in Oliver Goldsmith's (c. 1730–4) *Deserted Village* (1770). **689 sublunary:** of this earth.

747 hinds: estate workers. **753 scantling:** small amount. **751–4:** asset stripping to pay for gambling. **755–6 Estates are landscapes:** take on the fashionable transcience of paintings. **764–80 Improvement:** the eighteenth-century vogue for updating and 'beautifying' the design of country estates; equally fashionable, perhaps, was the literary habit of satirising such ambitions: see Pope in *Epistle to Burlington* or Austen in

Mansfield Park. **766 Brown:** Lancelot 'Capability' (1716–83), doyen of garden landscapers, had remodelled the nearby grounds of Castle Ashby for the Earl of Northampton, and, according to *Cowper Illustrated*, had laid out parts of Weston Park. **779 cascades:** a series of waterfalls.

835 thou: London. **836 complexions:** skin colours. **838 admire:** wonder at, with surprise rather than approval. **839 fair:** usually, a woman.

From Book IV: The Winter Evening 1 bridge: a long structure of twenty-four arches, at irregular distances, which joined Olney and Emberton. **6 frozen locks:** the winter of 1783–4 was said to be the worst for almost fifty years. **19 periods:** sentences. **23 budget:** bag, or its contents. **25–7:** American War of Independence had ended at the Treaty of Versailles (1783). **28–30:** Cowper was persistently hostile to colonial exploitation in India. **30–5:** parliamentary debates on India filled the newspapers of the winter of 1783. **49 placemen:** those who bought office with unquestioning support. **53 the fair:** women.

90 Babel: Genesis xi. **107 expatiates:** wanders at large. **114–9:** allusion to Cowper's fondness for travel books.

327 lapse: a gentle fall. **329 Assimilate:** blend into one. **349 consolidated:** frozen. **364 spleen:** causing depression.

540 lappets: ribbons attached to head-dress. **546 French heels:** elaborate high heels. **554 vestal:** virgin.

From Book V: The Winter Morning Walk 11 spindling: growing thin, attentuated, as in 'spindle-shanks'. **22 bents:** stiff-stemmed grasses. **29 unrecumbent:** standing. **40 Deciduous:** falling. **43 wedge:** for splitting logs. **46 lurcher:** sheepdog/greyhound cross. **52 churl:** rural labourer. **55 short tube:** tobacco pipe. **58 pale:** enclosure. **76 retrench'd:** reduced. **90 earth-nut:** a tuber, also known as 'pig-nut'. **94 nauseous dole:** a gift of food found in dung or vomit. **98 Indurated:** hard. **108 embroider'd:** frozen spray. **115 pellucid:** transparent. **129 Imperial mistress:** Empress Anna Ivanovna had built, in 1740, an ice-palace on the River Neva at St Petersburg. **135 Aristæus:** in Greek mythology he pursued Eurydice who accidentally was bitten by a snake; in punishment, the gods killed his bees. When he turned to his mother, Cyrene, for help, she parted the waters so that he could enter her palace beneath the River Peneus in Thessaly. **153 lambent:** a light or flame that consumes no fuel.

382 that of old: the Israelites enslaved in Egypt. **383 aveng'd:** Egyptians drowned in the Red Sea. **Bastile:** the storming of the prison in 1789 would herald the end of the tyrannies of the *ancien régime*.

From Book VI: The Winter Walk at Noon For a walk over the same ground see Book I, 266–325. **59 Slant:** sloping. **66 th' embattled tow'r:** crenellated church-tower at Emberton, a mile to the south of Olney. **67 music:** church bells.

135 subtle: hard to trace. **lymph:** sap. **139 th' intestine tide:** internal stream. **145 aspiring:** rising. **152 the other tall:** according to Cowper's note, the guelder rose (or marsh elder). **158 sanguine:** red. **162 woodbine:** honeysuckle. **165 Hypericum:** St John's wort. **167 Mezerion:** spurge laurel, or daphne; the flowers appear before the leaves. **170 Althæa:** marsh mallow. **179 fleecy load:** snow.

226–7 in whose sight: cf. Psalms 90:4, and Isaac Watts, 'Our God, our help in ages past'. **233 Pomona, Pales, Pan:** Roman goddesses of fruit trees and sheepfolds, Greek god of flocks and shepherds. **234 Flora and Vertumnus:** Roman goddess of flowers and gardens, Roman god of orchards, husband to Pomona. **242 inspires:** infuses, breathes into. **243 balmy:** fragrant, soothing.

295 sign: of the zodiac. **300 unwonted:** out of the habit of walking abroad. **302 king-cups:** marsh marigold. **303 prink:** decorate. **304 sallad:** watercress. **307 stock-dove:** wild pigeon. **315 flippant:** nimble and perhaps voluble. **334 kine:** cattle. **376 precipitate:** headlong. **398 resort:** places frequented by men. **399 delegate:** deputy. **415 crib:** barred receptacle for fodder. **420–4** the worrying and 'hunting' of cattle being driven to market was becoming an issue of concern to the London magistrates. **424 passenger:** passer-by.

562 sensibility: humanity, compassion. **567 reptile:** generally a 'creeping' animal; literally, it fits neither snail nor worm.

996 age of fabled gold: the age of innocence presided over by Saturn; see Ovid, *Metamorphoses*, I, 89–112.